Not Fit for a Dog!

The Truth About Manufactured Dog and Cat Food

Michael W. Fox, B.Vet. Med., Ph.D., D.Sc., M.R.C.V.S
Elizabeth Hodgkins, D.V.M
Marion E. Smart, D.V.M. Ph.D.

Quill Driver Books

Fresno, California

Printed in the United States of America.

Published by
Quill Driver Books, an imprint of Linden Publishing
2006 South Mary, Fresno, CA 93721
559-233-6633 / 800-345-4447
QuillDriverBooks.com

Quill Driver Books may be purchased for educational, fund-raising, business or promotional use. Please contact Special Markets, Quill Driver Books, at the above address or phone numbers.

Quill Driver Books Project Cadre:
June Clark, Doris Hall, Linda Kay Hardie,
Christine Hernandez, Dave Marion, Stephen Blake Mettee, Monica Stevens, Kent Sorsky

First Printing

ISBN 978-1-61035-149-2

To order a copy of this book, please call
1-800-345-4447.

Library of Congress Cataloging-in-Publication Data

Fox, Michael W., 1937-
Not fit for a dog! : the truth about manufactured dog and cat food /
by Michael W. Fox, Elizabeth Hodgkins, and Marion E. Smart.
p. cm.
ISBN 978-1-61035-149-2
1. Pet food industry. I. Hodgkins, Elizabeth M. II. Smart, Marion E.,
1944- III. Title.
HD9340.A2F69 2008
338.4'766466—dc22

2008003481

Contents

Foreword

When I qualified as a veterinarian in 1973, I left veterinary college believing I could cure almost all the patients I would meet during my veterinary career. It soon became apparent that I was wrong: So many dogs and cats with so much chronic disease, and so many drugs that didn't cure, or caused serious side effects.

After some years I discovered there were other treatments for pets—acupuncture, herbal medicine, homeopathy—and all these became new and effective therapies. But still I had patients that didn't respond completely, and—more to the point—I was seeing ever-increasing numbers of pets suffering from inflammatory bowel disease, eczema, diabetes and urinary tract infections that needed to be cured. What was the cause of all this chronic disease, and why, despite my best efforts, did some patients respond poorly to treatment?

Eventually—and by this time I had been practicing veterinary medicine for twenty years—I realized the root cause of most of these diseases. Something so simple, so obvious. Diet. The food that my patients were eating was making them ill.

Looking back now, it seems amazing that it took so long for me to realize that feeding dogs and cats day in, day out, on processed foods, laden with carbohydrates, would damage their health. Carbohydrates are not natural foodstuffs for cats, or for dogs as their main food. Processed pet foods are not healthy foods. They have artificial colorings, artificial flavorings, preservatives, peculiar-sounding ingredients such as "animal digest," "mechanically retrieved meat"—in fact, one quick look at the ingredients is enough to sound warning bells for anyone endowed with a modicum of common sense.

Once I began to suggest natural, healthy diets for my patients, their health began to improve. Many clients found it a little odd when I advised throwing away their bags of kibble and cans of cat food. But most of them saw the sense of feeding their pets "real" food. Just what their pets would eat in the wild.

If only I had understood the importance of a natural healthy diet for pets twenty or thirty years ago, how much more I could have helped my patients. So why didn't I? The book you are about to read, had it been available then, would have saved me decades of misunderstanding the fundamental relationship between natural healthy nutrition and a vibrant healthy pet.

Not Fit for a Dog! highlights the dangers of modern pet food—how it is unbalanced, creates addiction, and often contains ingredients that can literally poison your pet. It explodes the myths propounded by pet food companies that human food is "bad" for pets, and that natural diets are unsafe. It exposes the horrific truths that pet food manufacturers will sell you a 'normal' diet for your cat that will cause diabetes, and then sell you another prescription diet to help control the diabetes, and how prescription diets themselves can cause illness.

This book is a massive indictment of the pet food industry, but also of our whole approach to growing and processing food—for us humans as well as for our pets.

I asked the question: why didn't I realize for so long the dangers of manufactured pet food, and the benefits of a natural diet? The reason is that veterinary students are not given the facts. Indeed, information and training in pet nutrition for veterinary students is given, funded and controlled to a huge extent by the pet food industry itself.

If this book had been available when I was a student and a newly qualified vet, it would have transformed my attitude to nutrition and health for pets. If I was able, I would lock every veterinary student and every practicing veterinarian in a room with a copy of this book, and not let them out until they had read it from cover to cover.

RICHARD ALLPORT B.Vet.Med., M.R.C.V.S.
Potters Bar, Hertfordshire, England

Introduction

The pet food recall in spring 2007—the biggest pet food recall ever, that caused the untimely deaths of an estimated 8,500 cats and dogs across North America—brought three concerned veterinarians together to write this book and share with pet owners, other veterinarians, and animal-care providers their professional expertise and opinions on what is best to feed companion animals for their ultimate health and happiness.

Feeding one's pet is an important ritual for cat and dog owners because giving food is one of the most effective ways to express affection and appreciation and affirm the bond between the animal and the human care giver.

The sanctity of this fundamental part of the human-companion animal bond includes the trust that pet owners have in the various brands and varieties of commercial processed pet foods, often recommended by their veterinarians, that they feed every day to their beloved dogs and cats. Most pet owners trust veterinarians to put first and foremost the overall health and well-being of the clients' animal companions.

But the same cannot be said of the pet food industry that is a subsidiary of the multinational human food industry—an agribusiness enterprise with considerable political influence—that puts profits first. It has turned the recycling of human food and agricultural byproducts and wastes into a multibillion dollar business. While it is highly profitable, is it nutritious? Is it safe? We believe the answer is no.

The massive recall of more than 1,000 different varieties of cat and dog food is but the tip of the proverbial iceberg. At deeper levels, beneath the radar of inadequate government oversight, are serious problems when it comes to pet (and human) food manufacturers' claims and assurances of safety and quality. As this book reveals—even disregarding the poison-contaminated pet food ingredients bought on the cheap from China by American pet food manufacturers and suppliers—cats and dogs fed conventional manufactured pet foods are more likely to suffer chronic and costly quality of life issues at their owners' expense and anguish.

Feeding our pets a variety of nutritious, wholesome, safe foods appropriate for the individual species—for instance, cats are carnivores, and cannot ever be vegetarians—is a basic duty and fulfills an obligation we assume when we chose to own animals.

To some, this is sentimentalism and an unconscionable ideal when there is so much human poverty and malnutrition in the world. But the two are connected, as is the suffering of millions of sick, starving, poisoned, and dying dogs and cats in the third world. The dynamic is more rich versus poor, rather than pets versus people. As Mahatma Gandhi once said, "The cattle of the rich steal the bread of the poor."

At the impoverished end of the global market food chain, dogs and cats, along with other domestic animals, suffer many illnesses due in large part to dietary immunodeficiency. Dietary deficiencies mean weakened immune systems for humans and other animals. At the more affluent, if not conspicuously consumptive, end of the food chain, cats and dogs mirror many of the diseases of dietary excess and imbalance evident in their owners, notably obesity, diabetes, heart disease, various forms of cancer, arthritis, allergies, digestive disorders, and other diet-related health problems. These two poles of the global food market are connected by the politics of market access, multinational corporate hegemony and monopoly, declining food quality and affordability, and the searing legacies of colonialism, land misuse, and population growth.

Hunger and malnutrition are interwoven in both humans and other animals even in the absence of poverty. Animals can be malnourished and suffer from one or more nutrition-related diseases even though they are being fed all they can eat. This has more to do with the economics of what is in the commercial processed food than with nutritional genomics.

The bulk ingredients of so-called "scientifically formulated and balanced" diets for dogs and cats are primarily highly pro-

NUTRITIONAL GENOMIC RESEARCH

After scientists mapped the human genome, they turned to dogs, then to cats. As they uncover the secrets of companion animals' genes, the natural next step is nutritional genomic research. This research will provide information to formulate pet foods according to the animals' genetic needs, rather than more or less by trial and error with feeding tests.

cessed agricultural, livestock, and food and beverage industry wastes. Consumers see these termed "byproduct" and "meal" (like poultry byproduct and meat meal) on attractively designed "gourmet" and "premium" pet food labels.

Most processed commercial pet foods contain virtually no whole food ingredients such as rice, oats, and barley, but processed fractions, such as bran, gluten, starch, and other milling process byproducts. Ingredients consisting of animal protein, usually listed as byproducts or meal, are likewise of dubious nutritional value, and until recently even hydrolyzed poultry feathers, along with beaks and claws, were included as part of the animal protein content. When it says "meat" on the label, your guess is as good as ours; the "meat" could be from animals such as pigs or horses that many people would find offensive for religious or cultural reasons, and in recent times, even the recycled remains of dogs and cats have gone under this ubiquitous label!

The majority of ingredients listed on the label are actually synthetic chemicals. These include various vitamins, minerals, amino acids, and other supplements that are added because these essential nutrients are missing from the highly processed material that becomes manufactured pet food and livestock feed. Preservatives (antioxidants), stabilizers, coloring agents, taste and texture enhancers are also usually listed, but not the chemicals lining the container (notably bisphenols), plus the various chemical residues in ingredients subjected to various extraction and other processes, including infusion with ethoxyquin (quinoline-based antioxidant) to prevent rancidity.

This chemical feast for pets is based on the simplistic nutritional science developed for cost effectively feeding animals farmed by the livestock industry, that sector of agribusiness that relies on the pet-owning public (whose animal bond they promote and exploit) to recycle the inedible and condemned remains of diseased, dead, debilitated, and dying farmed animals, termed 4-D meat by the meat processors. It is a simplistic science based on percentages of fat, protein, carbohydrate, fiber, and ash, that has gotten the pet food industry in trouble repeatedly over the years. In many cases, after making extravagant claims that a given food is complete and balanced, the pet food industry has had to correct problems that caused nutrition-related diseases, such as taurine deficiency or essential fatty acid deficiency.

In this book you will learn:

- How to read pet food labels, and what you need to avoid for your pets' sake.
- How to save on vet bills by preventing your animal from developing diet-related diseases.
- Why your vet may not have much to say about pet foods.
- Why cats are more at risk from dry pet foods than dogs.
- What diet-related diseases your animal may already have, and how a change in diet can help.
- How our health and our pets' health are interconnected.
- Why we should all support organic farming practices and suppliers.

Just and Equitable Choices

The morality of providing good nutrition to a pet while children around the world are malnourished and starving is an issue of conscience that will not be resolved until there is a bioethical foundation for agriculture, and until the inequities of "free" trade and the associated marginalization of social justice and human rights, animal welfare, and environmental protection and restoration are corrected, especially regarding global food quality and security.

Gandhi wrote that "...it is an insult to a starving dog to throw a crumb to him. Roving dogs do not indicate the civilization or compassion of the society; they betray on the contrary the ignorance and lethargy of its members." We do not believe that he specifically meant India or any other third world nation, but the world community where money rules, and ignorance and indifference prevail, more so today than ever.

Part of the solution to starving, free-roaming dogs—and to world hunger—does not mean poisoning all the free-roaming dogs, or prohibiting affluent people from keeping pets and feeding them well, or in making them feel guilty for doing so. It lies in pet owners joining with other consumers in support of a socially just, equitable, healthful, and affordable food chain that is ecologically sound, sustainable, regenerative, humane, and organically certified. Such civil society initiatives as community-supported agriculture and market cooperatives, support for locally grown and prepared foods, including pet foods (or making these at home), are enlightened choices for not only the health-conscious, but for all people of conscience.

In fact, the pets of the industrial world do not steal the bread of the poor. Besides hunting and killing for themselves, dogs and cats in poor countries recycle inedible and discarded food items from the community garbage piles. Those in the West, and other affluent parts of the world, recycle waste byproducts from the agribusiness food industry community. Neither of these dietary regimens provides these animals with optimal nutrition. Certainly the scavenging dog or cat is not as well nourished as the one being fed manufactured processed pet foods, but it would be wrong to claim that any consistent standard of optimal nutrition has been achieved in any developed country for consumers and their animal companions. The contents of most widely advertised dry cat foods—and breakfast cereals for children—support this conclusion. It is also a fact that organically grown crops and products from farmed animals fed organically certified feeds are safer and contain more nutrients than conventional "Green Revolution" crop varieties, and also the so-called "Doubly Green" (genetically engineered) crop varieties, the quality and safety of which are now in doubt. But organically certified food is not only higher priced, it is a threat to the petrochemical and biotechnology industry sectors of "agribusiness" that continue to garner political support and lucrative public subsidies.

It has taken a long time for the pet-owning public and the veterinary profession to wake up and see through all the pet food advertising hype to the connection between the health of people eating a processed- and prepared-food diet, and the similar health problems in cats and dogs on a daily diet of entirely processed, denatured, adulterated food industry wastes, along with a cocktail of chemical additives and contaminants.

It has been said that the more one has to hide, the more one displays to the contrary. This is precisely what the commercial pet food industry does, putting, as a rule, far more ingredient content information on pet food labels than do most human food manufacturers. The manufactured convenience foods for people and their pets are said to be "science based" in their formulation, according to the multinational agribusiness oligopoly. But when diet- and nutrition-associated diseases are put into the equation, the evidence shows that corporate profits and profits to the medical/pharmaceutical industry outweigh considerations of consumers and their pets.

Finding pure and wholesome food—and water—is a challenge today. But we must all make the effort and demand and support more healthful farming practices and dietary choices and habits, including what we feed our animal companions.

Chapter 1

An Introduction to What You Are Feeding Your Pet

In the beginning, nutrition was simple: it was a matter of survival. When people entered the picture, packs of wolf-like dogs found that they could more easily stave off hunger by following nomadic human hunters who would lead them to food or even leave food scraps behind as they went. This relationship eventually became mutually beneficial when the dog realized that in return for a few simple tasks such as guarding the home, finding and retrieving game, and herding other animals, humans were willing to share their food and the warmth of the fire.

Later the cat found that leaving its lifestyle as a solitary hunter and joining people had benefits. Living on or near a farm brought shelter and a consistent supply of rodents as the cat patrolled and unwittingly protected man's winter supply of food.

Over the centuries these relationships have become more interdependent. Dogs were easily domesticated and bred to fulfill various roles within the human society, and cats left their predatory role and entered a new domesticated environment where they were more dependent on the humans. As our society and our diets have changed, so has what we feed our pets and what we expect from them. As a result, nutrition for companion animals has become more complex.

The Commercial Pet Food Industry

Today, nutrition for pet dogs and cats looks a lot like nutrition for people. The commercial pet food industry appears to offer an unlimited and diverse number of brands and types of food sold in grocery stores, pet specialty stores, and veterinary clinics. This impression is deceptive, because only seven companies account for

86 percent of the market share in the United States. In Canada 75 percent of the pet food sold is manufactured in the United States.

These few multinational companies extensively research and carefully orchestrate their marketing and sales strategies. This has a large influence on what people consider good nutrition and the kinds of pet food the public buys. Marketing and sales departments are on the constant lookout for new trends or popular topics that can help sell more or more expensive pet food. As a result, foods are marketed as breed-specific, life-stage-specific, premium, ultra-premium, and organic.

The marketing focus includes:

- the expansion of premium diets and "healthy" treats and snacks—from 1996 to 2002 the number of products labeled "organic" or "natural" doubled;
- diets that address special pet needs such as joints, teeth, coat, etc.;
- specific small-breed and large-breed dog requirements for growth and maintenance;
- increasing palatability and maintenance of freshness;
- packaging and convenience for the pet owner;
- enhancing intelligence;
- increasing longevity, including maintaining the quality of life for pets with life-threatening or terminal diseases;
- designing diets based on genomic research; and
- introducing "functional foods," which are foods or dietary components that may provide health benefit beyond basic nutrition.

These products take advantage of trends in human diets and the fact that most people consider their pets as members of the family to sell their trendy but not necessarily nutritious highly processed foods.

Small Pet Food Makers

In addition to the large pet food manufacturers, a growing number of small pet food makers are attracting people who want the best for their pet and are concerned about the long-term health impact of feeding commercial dry (kibble) and canned food to their pets. These smaller companies usually produce raw, frozen, dehydrated, or baked whole food diets that are more expensive, but claim to have healthier and more natural ingredients. Many makers are devoted dog breeders and have had their kennels on these diets for several generations prior to making the diets available to the public. These whole food diets presently account for approximately 10 percent of North American pet food sales, but because of consumer awareness and perception that these are safer, sales are predicted to grow into the high double digits over the next two years.

Raw pet food manufacturers are particularly singled out by the multinational pet food corporations and the veterinary profession. The main claim against such diets is that raw diets represent a significant public health risk, with the possibility of parasites, bacteria, and other problems being spread through uncooked ingredients. Another major complaint is that the basic nutritional concept of these diets is flawed. Manufacturers say the diets are not necessarily balanced in each particular batch, but are balanced over time, meaning any dietary deficiency in one recipe would be corrected by subsequently including other ingredients. This is questionable, as there is no solid research to back it.

Most manufacturers of raw diets are aware of this, but for most, their basic knowledge of nutrition is solid as reflected on their websites. Scientists and veterinarians may argue that the claim "balanced over time" is an inappropriate concept, and that at best the evidence in support of these diets is anecdotal. But as solid as the nutritional data is for many of these raw-food makers, as more jump on the bandwagon in this booming field, there is an increasing danger of foods being sold without solid nutrition and a growing chance of problems due to the health risks associated with contamination in raw foods.

In the face of these concerns, some of the small raw food manufacturers have responded by putting in place strict quality control measures:

- They have contracts with livestock and poultry producers who supply them with healthy cull animals.
- These animals are slaughtered at a federally inspected plant.
- The carcass or salvageable organs are chilled, transported to the manufacturing plant, processed into the final product in a cold room, and immediately frozen.
- In the United States, they must comply with Food and Drug Administration standards, and in Canada, they are certified by, and are open to, Canadian Food Inspection Agency inspections.
- The diets are independently analyzed.

These diets, when sold through a commercial outlet, are subject to the same label requirements, recalls, and regulations as the rest of the commercial pet food industry.

This is a niche but growing market and it is limited to some extent by availability of acceptable animals and an appropriate local slaughterhouse, and the energy expenditure associated with transportation and storage.

At present, the multinationals are only attempting to mimic these products with cooked foods. While each has the ingredients and production capabilities of mass-producing these diets, at present this would not be economically feasible both from the companies' and the consumers' perspectives.

The Veterinary Profession: The Public Perception

The public believes that veterinarians have a strong nutritional background upon graduation. This perception is fueled by the pet food industry, which spends around $400 million on advertising in the United States alone, often to tout that their products are recommended by veterinarians.

Additional money is spent on brochures, websites, and attractive packaging (the latter often falls under the category of Research & Development in a company's ledgers). Still, the phrase "recommended by veterinarians" has no defined meaning. Potentially it could mean anything from "every single veterinarian in the world recommends this product" to "we found two veterinarians who would agree to recommend this product," with the truth probably lying somewhere in between.

Since there is very little regulation on the information that the pet food industry produces and distributes, pet owners' sensibilities are often overwhelmed by the multitude of claims and confusing information. For example, now that glucosamine (for joint protection) has become a popular buzz word, suddenly poultry byproduct meal has been transformed by one large manufacturer into poultry byproduct meal, a natural source of glucosamine. Yes, it is the same old meal, but now the glucosamine in the ground-up bone has lifted it to a more valuable status.

Because of this confusion, pet owners often turn to their veterinarians for dietary advice. This isn't too surprising since virtually all governmental or commercial material on the subject suggests that owners do just that.

Veterinarians have a great influence on the decisions made by their clients concerning the diets fed to their pets. This relationship is somewhat unique within the medical community; a medical doctor will often refer his patient to a dietician or nutritionist if substantial dietary intervention is required. Veterinarians not only advise their clients on what to feed their healthy pets, but also sell veterinary prescription diets to manage or treat specific health problems. During a typical day, a veterinarian is as likely to give nutritional advice as pharmaceutical advice, yet in the veterinary curriculum on average there are fewer than twenty hours of companion animal nutrition lectures compared to more than sixty hours on veterinary pharmaceuticals.

With this small amount of nutritional education, can a veterinarian actually provide positive factual, unbiased advice in the face of this advertising and marketing onslaught? With hundreds of new diets and diet-related supplements released annually, each one promising to embrace the latest innovative concepts in pet nutrition, how can a veterinarian keep up and remain knowledgeable without becoming a victim to the same promotional advertising that the pet owner is questioning?

What Do Veterinarians Know about Nutrition?

In the veterinary curriculum, nutrition has traditionally been taught by animal scientists with a focus primarily on livestock feed identification and ration formulation. The only other exposure a veterinary student has to nutrition is during pathology, toxicology, and medicine lectures. The student learns the basic clinical signs of nutritional diseases. Unfortunately, these lectures are often lost in the hours spent on what schools and teachers consider real veterinary problems, such as medicine and surgery. Although the curriculum in most veterinary colleges has shifted emphasis from food animal production to companion animals, the emphasis on nutrition is still small compared to how important it is.

The American College of Veterinary Nutrition was established in 1988. To accelerate the training of nutrition to veterinary students, its curriculum committee outlined a standard of training and core competencies for veterinary professionals. The idea was to provide schools with uniform nutritional education standards to be included within the core curriculum. To date, some colleges are utilizing this approach. In a 2006 survey, twenty-eight accredited veterinary colleges had between one- and three-credit courses in basic nutrition during the first two years of their program.

A survey done in 2007 by the Veterinary Information Network found that although nutrition was taught in most undergraduate curriculums, 53 percent of the courses spent less than 20 percent of the time on feline and canine nutrition. One study showed that 76 percent of veterinarians felt that their undergraduate training had not prepared them to deal with the huge Menu Foods recalls (see Chapter 2).

The Pet Food Industry Fills the Education Cracks

Since, in most veterinary colleges, companion animal nutrition has historically fallen through the cracks, the pet food industry generously has offered to fill in. Academia has welcomed their input for several reasons:

- The offer includes providing free extracurricular lectures and labs in companion animal nutrition, which do not interfere with an established timetable or drain an academic budget, as companion animal nutrition is taught without the need for trained faculty.

- Free or discounted pet foods are offered to the student, faculty, and staff.
- To support and organize the company's undergraduate programs within each college, a student coordinator is hired (which provides financial aid to these students).
- Free or discounted prescription diets are made available to teaching hospitals to be sold with any profits going to benefit the school.
- Free or discounted pet foods are made available to university animal resource centers to feed the research cats and dogs.
- New research monies are made available for small animal clinicians to do research and develop graduate programs in a traditionally underfunded discipline.
- Financial support can include sponsoring a faculty chair, special equipment, or hospital improvements.

In the past, the university and a pet food company negotiated a contract that allowed the pet food company exclusivity. Now the contracts are less binding as more pet food manufacturers participate.

How Did this Situation Develop?

In 1976, Colgate-Palmolive acquired a small pet food producer named Hill's Pet Products. Based on its experience with using dentists to promote its toothpastes (and similar successes in the pharmaceutical and tobacco industries), Colgate decided to have veterinarians endorse its Science Diet pet food line. Hill's Science Diet obtained these endorsements by providing free pet food to vet students, by funding hundreds of thousands of dollars of research at each of the twenty-seven U.S. veterinary colleges, and funding nutrition professorships at many veterinary schools. "The bulk of our expenditure went to the veterinary community," said a former Colgate's senior vice president of global marketing and sales.

The success of this strategy is clear: With a fraction of the marketing budget of its competitors, Hill's grew from a company with $40 million in sales in 1982 to the fourth-largest producer of pet food in the world with $1.5 billion in net sales and an operating profit of $412 million. This success inspired other major players in the industry to imitate its strategies, and this approach remains a standard today.

Many people within and outside the profession feel this relationship is not ethical and that, when the full extent of it is realized, the reputation of the veterinary profession will be compromised. The question arises: How can one justify supporting an industry that reacted to a problem it created through the diets it developed and marketed (i.e., nutritionally-related diseases) by producing and marketing expensive special diets rather than pulling the offending products off the market?

The Evolution of the Modern Pet Food Industry

Canned dog food opened its lid in the 1920s. A large number of pet foods burst into the market later with the introduction of extrusion, a method of cooking and processing ingredients into a digestible, palatable, and sterile dry food, commonly referred to as kibble. Before this, dry dog foods were formed into pellets or baked in a much more labor-intensive procedure.

From the mid-1950s to the mid-1980s, the demand for commercial pet foods, sold through feed stores and supermarkets, increased rapidly. Today more than 15,000 different brands are sold in the United States and Canada. One large high-tech private label company produces more than 500 formulations sold under no fewer than 1,200 different labels, but sells none under its own label. At one time, the only pet treat sold in the market was a dry dog biscuit; now one finds it hard to decide what type of treat to buy.

Canned foods have changed from the large tin cans containing primarily meat with 60 percent to 78 percent moisture to smaller, more convenient packages, with balanced nutrients, less meat and higher moisture (78 percent to 82 percent).

The Rendering Industry

The rendering industry is critical to an efficient, sustainable agricultural industry. This industry takes products not needed or suitable for human consumption from the vegetable, grain, and meat processing plants and produces a large variety of byproducts for animal consumption. About 50 percent of beef, 44 percent of swine, and 30 percent of poultry tissues are not destined to be used in human food, and this produces 47 billion pounds of waste materials per year, 23 percent of which goes into pet foods. The animal tissues prior to rendering have a moisture content of 50 to 90 percent; this moisture is removed by rendering to produce meal.

The Evolution of the Knowledge of Nutrient Requirements for Dogs

As early as 1949, the veterinary literature contained nutritional information that is applicable today. The National Research Council committee on canine and feline nutrition first published its recommendations in 1972. These recommendations were based on a review and an interpretation of the scientific research about small animal nutrition. In this publication, 34 percent of the scientific references were published prior to 1950.

Early research was done on dogs serving as animal models for human nutritional studies. Most of the tests involved purified or semi-purified diets that lacked specific nutrients or contained them in toxic concentrations. Now, most of the large manufacturers of commercial dog foods have their own research kennels where they study primarily the palatability of their formulations against the competition, since better tasting foods sell better.

Independent research kennels also test dog foods following criteria established by the Association of American Feed Control Officials. One of the present concerns is whether these AAFCO criteria apply suitably to all the breeds and levels of activity of our dogs.

Dogs represent a diverse population of animals, with a large number of functions from lap companions to heavy workers. Over the last 100 years, the physical criteria used by breeders to select champion breeding stock have changed. Altered genetics not only change the physical characteristics but also can alter the animal metabolism. Various breeds of dogs may have their own special requirements depending on their genetic make-up and function. Line breeding has resulted in dogs that metabolize nutrients in abnormal ways. For example, the Bedlington terrier cannot release copper from its liver and Irish setters are wheat-sensitive. Special diets may be required to maintain the health of these pets.

Evaluating a Pet Food

In commercially manufactured pet foods, most of the ingredients are byproducts of the agricultural industry from the production of human food. "Human grade ingredients" is a term often used in the promotion of pet foods, but this term has little meaning. For one thing, as soon as a product leaves the slaughterhouse and enters a pet food plant it is no longer considered suitable for human consumption.

Another misconception is that the ingredient sources in veterinary prescription diets are superior to those used in commercial pet foods. If the manufacturing plant produces both acceptable quality commercial diets and prescription diets, then the ingredients used in both are likely from the same source and quality. Most of the ingredients arrive at the pet food manufacturing plant as a dried meal from a distributor or a broker who has purchased the ingredient from a rendering plant or slaughterhouse or on the commodity market using the criteria specified by the pet food manufacturer.

If chicken or meat is the first ingredient on the food label, the consumer may perceive that the diet is of higher quality than one where a plant protein or an animal meal is listed as the first ingredient. In order for chicken or meat to be listed first, it must occupy at least 15 percent of the formula. When including chicken in the formulation, fat content is as important as the protein content and may contribute more than 15 percent of the dietary fat. The digestibility of whole meat is slightly better than the meals primarily because it has been cooked only once.

The choice of a pet food ingredient is not only dependent on its nutrient content but also on its functional qualities such as water-holding capacity and collagen solubility. Twenty years of advances in extrusion technology (kibble making) have now accommodated for the added moisture and fat in the conditioning chambers of the extruder. These are related to the physical appearance of the kibble when the pet's human companion opens the bag. Since humans are the ones buying the food, it must look good to them.

Required Nutrients

What they do

Nutrients are used by the body in many ways:

- In the growth and maintenance of structural components such as bone
- For metabolism
- For the regulation of body temperature
- To maintain gestation and lactation
- To provide energy for work
- To maintain an optimal immune system
- To prevent or combat disease
- For tissue repair

The main ingredients in a diet provide the primary nutrients required by a dog or cat.

Protein

Protein comes from meat, meat byproducts, or plant byproducts. Once digested, dietary protein provides amino acids, which act as building blocks for new proteins for all living cells, and are used to regulate metabolism and growth and to repair tissue. The proteins in the diet must contain the essential (those that cannot be manufactured by the body) and non-essential amino acids (those that can be synthesized by the body from an excess of other dietary amino acids or from other sources of dietary nitrogen). The quality of protein depends on the balance of the essential amino acids. To balance the amino acid profiles of the poorer quality protein sources, pet food manufacturers add the deficient amino acids to the diet. Lysine, methionine, and cystine are the amino acids most often added.

Heat sensitive amino acids are destroyed during the extrusion process and are sprayed on again with fat just before the product is bagged.

Animal-based sources for protein can vary in quality, nutrient digestibility and bioavailability related to the amount of bone, collagen, and cartilage present in proportion to the amount of striated muscle. Plant-based protein sources are more consistent in nutrient levels but lacking in some of the essential amino acids.

Fat

Fat, a concentrated source of energy, provides the body with essential fatty acids and is a carrier for the fat-soluble vitamins A, D, E, and K. Dietary sources of fat are saturated, unsaturated, and polyunsaturated. The essential fatty acids, linoleic (omega-6), alpha-linolenic (omega-3) and arachidonic, are all polyunsaturated. Fatty acids are an important component of cell walls, and are involved in reproduction, the inflammatory process, and the immune system as well as maintaining a healthy skin and hair coat. Diets high in polyunsaturated fatty acids can become rancid if an antioxidant such as vitamin E, ethoxyquin or butyrate hydroxytoluen (BHT) is not added.

Carbohydrates

Dietary carbohydrates provide the body with energy, and any excess is converted to body fat and glycogen. Carbohydrate sources, primarily grains or, on occasion, starchy vegetables, contain a mixture of simple (glucose) and complex (starch) sugars. Carbohydrates are not essential to pets—especially cats—as they can synthesize enough glucose to meet their metabolic needs from amino acids and glycerol provided by the proteins and fat in their diet. Dietary carbohydrates, and not fat, may be the main contributor to obesity seen as an epidemic in pets today (see Chapters 7 through 9 for more details).

Fiber

Dietary fiber or roughage in the diet, composed of indigestible cellulose, pectin, and lignin, provides bulk to the stool and helps keep your pet regular. Fiber has become part of our everyday conversation as Baby Boomers age. This is a fact that has not escaped the notice of pet food manufacturers.

Fructooligosaccharides (FOS), a soluble fiber, has become popular as a prebiotic supplier of nutrients to bacteria found naturally in the intestinal tract. FOS is found as inulin in tubers, roots, and fruit such as chicory, onions, bananas, and artichokes, and is composed primarily of fructose.

FOS can only be broken down by bacteria found in the intestines and are utilized by the colonic bacteria to shift the bacterial population to bifidobacterium and lactobacillus. These bacteria increase the lactic and butyric acids which fuel the colonocytes (special protective cells found in the colon) to make the intestinal tract environment less inviting to harmful organisms. One percent FOS in a diet reduces fecal odor, but as little as 6 percent FOS can negatively affect digestibility and intestinal health. A healthy growing bacterial population needs ammonia (a byproduct of protein digestion) and carbon to manufacturer their own amino acids. The net result is a decrease in the ammonia that is present in the colon, thus reducing its absorption and conversion to urea that must be secreted by the kidneys.

Vitamins and Minerals

The diet must also provide a pet with adequate minerals and vitamins. These are primarily provided in a premix that is added to the diet during the mixing process, or is mixed with fat and sprayed on the final product before packaging. This is often promoted as balanced with a natural source of minerals and vitamins. The amount of minerals required in the diet is usually less than 1 percent. Minerals in the diet have a number of important functions:

- maintain the structure of bones and teeth
- transport oxygen to tissues

- maintain the response of nervous tissue
- support organ function and integrity
- support endocrine function
- maintain electrolyte and water balance
- promote blood clotting

Important macro-minerals are calcium, phosphorus, sodium, potassium, chlorine, magnesium, and sulfur. Important micro-minerals are iron, copper, zinc, iodine, manganese, and selenium.

Most commercial pet foods are balanced in minerals. Problems can arise when the pet owner supplements commercial diets with extra minerals. Genetics can alter the animal's ability to metabolize certain minerals; this is especially true in breeds with a small gene pool. The impaired-copper metabolism in Bedlington terriers and chondrodysplasic (joint and limb-deformed) Alaskan malamutes are examples.

Most vitamins are required by the body in small amounts, but their absence from the diet can have a major impact on normal metabolism. Fat-soluble vitamins A, D, E, and K are stored in the body. Water-soluble vitamin C, thiamine, niacin, biotin, folic acid, riboflavin, B_6, B_{12}, and pantothenic acid are readily excreted but not stored. Those vitamins the body cannot store must be in the food on a regular basis, while those that can be stored can be utilized from the body's reserves for some time if they are deficient in the diet. Nearly all commercial diets have a balanced vitamin mixture added to them that allows for losses that can occur during processing and storage of a diet.

Dietary Excesses, Deficiencies, and Supplements

Since many consumers take various vitamin and mineral supplements, they will also give them to their animal companions. But this may cause problems. Vitamin C is used as an antioxidant (preservative) in some pet foods and, if the daily intake is increased by giving the pet vitamin C supplements, liver and kidney disorders may develop, as may skeletal abnormalities in puppies. Unlike humans, dogs normally have no need of an external source of vitamin C since they are able to make this vitamin in their livers.

Vitamin C, present as ascorbic acid, can cause intestinal irritation and cause mineral loss when excess ascorbic acid is excreted in the urine. These problems are rectified when this vitamin is provided in the form of Ester-C, or calcium ascorbate, or magnesium ascorbate. Excessive supplementation with vitamin A can cause liver damage and decalcify bones and teeth.

Too much calcium supplementation can impair body uptake of copper, phosphorus, iron, and zinc. Calcium supplementation is often recommended for fast-growing puppies, especially of the giant breeds. But this is often ill-advised because many dog and cat foods contain from 20 percent to120 percent more calcium than the amount recommended by the National Research Council. This is because cheap ingredients, as noted on labels, like meat and poultry byproducts and meat and poultry byproduct meal, while giving pet owners the false impression that they are high in quality protein, are actually high in ground bone. This accounts for potentially harmful levels of calcium in some pet foods.

Excessive dietary calcium can cause crippling bone and joint disease (osteochondrosis), bone deformities, vertebral abnormalities with concurrent neurological complications (wobblers syndrome), and be a factor in hip dysplasia, various skeletal disorders (like eosinophilic panosteitis, osteochondritis dissecans, hypertrophic osteodystrophy), and decreased thyroid function. Excessive calcium in the diet can interfere with zinc absorption, leading to zinc deficiency. This can be manifested as dermatitis and loss of hair pigmentation, poor growth in puppies, impaired immunity, delayed healing, and other problems.

Some dog breeds prone to developing gastric bloat become more susceptible when their diets contain excessive amounts of calcium, especially in puppyhood, and even while in utero when their mothers are given calcium supplements. Excessive zinc supplementation interferes with calcium, phosphorus, and copper absorption. High levels of phosphorus and magnesium in ground-up bone meal mixed in with the meat or poultry meal can contribute to kidney disease, which is a common disorder in dogs and cats today.

Is there a Need for Additional Vitamins and Minerals?

The nutritional jury is still out on this question. Some supplements are regarded as a panacea for all health problems. One set of requirements will not be applicable to all the different dog and cat breeds. Many breeders with years of experience sometimes develop feeding strategies that the scientific community often regards as "folklore." When a breeder discusses these diets it may be best to remember this quote: "Nothing upsets a good theory like a little experience." So is there an answer? In a healthy non-stressed pet on an adequate diet, additional supplementation is not necessary. Supplementation under this condition may create mild to severe imbalances in the diet.

Supplementation may be recommended by a veterinarian to accommodate nutrient losses associated with specific metabolic requirements (pregnancy, trauma, surgery, etc.) or diseases (renal disease, gastrointestinal disease, pancreatitis, etc.). For these conditions, however, unsupervised supplementation is not recommended. The best advice is to use common sense and ask for help if questions arise.

Water

Water is essential for life. The pet receives water from three sources:

- Water produced by the body metabolism.
- Water derived from the diet. Dry diets are about 10 percent water, semi-moist diets contain 25 percent to 30 percent water, and canned diets run 70 percent to 82 percent water.
- Water consumed directly.

Water consumption can increase because of habits (say a dog likes to play in the water), salt in the animal's diet, physical or metabolic activity, the environmental temperature, and diseases that involve the gastrointestinal tract (vomiting, diarrhea), the kidneys, or the endocrine system (diabetes mellitus).

Water quality may not be as important to a pet's health as it is to ours. Pets often drink out of potholes or the toilet bowl, but we hope these are not an animal's primary source. Your pet's main source of water should be supplied fresh daily and be available at all times. Water that is safe for you to drink is safe for your pet.

Secondary Ingredients

Flavors

Before a pet will eat a nutritionally adequate diet, the food must smell (olfaction) and taste good (gustation) and have an acceptable texture (tactile). How these three senses are associated with palatability differs with individual animals and is influenced by breed, age, health status, medications being administered, and zinc status. Animals can develop an aversion to foods associated with a previous unpleasant feeding experience.

Millions of dollars are spent to develop the ultimate flavor, the one that will make your pet beg for more. The flavors must also be acceptable to you. A pet food that smells like cat feces will not be a big seller, but some dogs do like to lunch in the litter box. Most flavors are derived from fresh meat that is hydrolyzed to generate protein breakdown products. One dog food company uses miniature schnauzers to test the palatability of their diets, as they found beagles would eat almost anything. Great secrecy can surround a successful flavor because it gives a company a competitive edge.

There is a saying that applies to pet food and flavors: "Technology is like a steam roller. If you are not on it, then you are destined to become part of the road." An example of this technology is a flavor that passes through the dam's milk, meaning that the weaned young will easily turn to diets with the same flavor because of a comfort factor and a sense of familiarity. An older pet can have a decreased sense of smell and taste; thus geriatric diets will often contain enhanced flavors.

Antioxidants

Antioxidants are added to the diet to prevent the unsaturated fats from going rancid, thus increasing the shelf life of the product. These have no systemic benefits to the animal. When diets go rancid, offensive odors and toxins may be produced and essential nutrients can be destroyed.

Natural antioxidants such as vitamin C, vitamin E, and carotenoids, when added to prevent rancidity, are effective for only short periods of time. For longer periods, synthetic antioxidants are required. Some synthetic antioxidants are ethoxyquin, butyrate hydroxytoluene (BHT), and butyrate hydroxyanisole (BHA). Ethoxyquin is the most efficient of the synthetic antioxidants.

Dog breeders have implicated ethoxyquin as a cause in a wide variety of problems in their pets. To date, most of the evidence is circumstantial. Remember, any nutrient is toxic if taken in excess. Ethoxyquin has been removed from over-the-counter diets but is still included in some veterinary prescription diets.

What is meant by a "natural" antioxidant?

When a consumer sees the word "natural" describing a nutrient, visions of a pure, uncontaminated, and holistic product are conjured up. All antioxidants originate from carbon, sulfur, hydrogen, and oxygen. "Natural vitamin E" is manufactured from the residue of soybean oil. The vitamin E used to protect food (fat) from becoming rancid is in a different form than the vitamin E used in vitamin pills and has no protective function within the body. All antioxidants are chemically processed. The natural antioxidants retain only 20 percent of their activity through extrusion and storage. Ethoxyquin retains 85 percent of its activity.

Examples of some natural antioxidants are:

• Mixed tocopherols. These are isomers of vitamin E extracted from vegetable oils. The most effective is gamma-tocopherol derived from cereal grains and oils.

• Rosemary extract, extracted from the herb, prevents oxidation of unsaturated fatty acids and protects flavors.

• Citric acid (vitamin C).

Additives

Additives are nonnutritive substances added during the manufacturing of the ingredients or the diets in micro quantities to fulfill a specific need. Some of these needs are to prevent caking of the ingredients, to bind ingredients together to form a stable pellet, to increase diet palatability (flavors), to maintain a semi-moist condition (humectants), to add color and to increase the shelf life (preservatives, antioxidants). Additives can be inert and not digested while others may be digested and metabolized before the body excretes them. Some additives have come under criticism since large quantities fed over a period of time may be carcinogenic or produce other diseases. The United States Food and Drug Administration has investigated most additives, and they are generally regarded as safe.

Humectants

These additives are used in the production of semi-moist pet foods. Presently controversy exists about the use of propylene glycol. Propylene glycol is absorbed, with one-third excreted by the kidneys. At high oral intakes it may cause kidney injury, central nervous system depression, and Heinz body anemia in cats, and may be a predisposing factor in some cases of diabetes mellitus. In cats, one study showed that a diet containing 6 percent propylene glycol decreased red blood cell survival rate.

Nutraceuticals, Prebiotics, and Probiotics

Nutraceuticals are products designed for specific health benefits and fit into a category between a nutritional product and a drug. These range from isolated nutrients, dietary supplements, genetically engineered foods, herbal products, and processed foods. Japan is the leader in the development and manufacturing of these products.

Prebiotics are food substances intended to promote the growth of beneficial microorganisms within the intestines. As mentioned, fructooligosaccharides are promoted in pet foods as a soluble fiber that promotes and maintains a microbial population in the colon, nourishing and keeping the colonocytes healthy. Probiotics are beneficial microorganisms, including lactobacillus and bifidobacterium. In addition, yeasts are added to the diet to aid in digestion and maintain a healthy intestinal flora. One of the common promotional features of premium diets is that they may contain prebiotics and/or probiotics.

Common Pet Food Problems

Mycotoxins

These are produced by fungi that contaminate grains grown, harvested, or stored under unfavorable environmental conditions such as high moisture that favor their growth. These toxins are not intentionally added to the diet and most companies test grains, if any of the hazardous conditions exist, for mycotoxin production. Mycotoxins can be harmless, reduce diet palatability, cause hormonal imbalances, lead to organ failure, or be carcinogenic. Sixteen thousand tons of pet food was recalled in 1995 by one manufacturer because it contained a high concentration of mycotoxins.

Anti-Nutritional/Anti-Quality Factors

Feed ingredients can contain allelochemicals, which may have a negative impact on animal health. These allelochemicals are primarily in plant-derived ingredients and include trypsin and amylase enzyme inhibitors, tannins, oxalates, glucosinolates, phytates, estrogens, and alkaloids. These natural chemicals can result in impaired growth, feed consumption, and efficiency of feed utilization, alterations in normal metabolism, fetal abnormalities, and increased nutrient requirements of essential amino acids, vitamins, and minerals. The agricultural-feed industry is aware of these problems and has developed measures aimed at reducing the concentrations and anti-nutritive effects with new processing techniques, dietary additives, and by altering the plant genetics.

MAD-COW DISEASE

There is concern that diets fed to our pets contain the prion (a protein particle smaller than a virus) that causes mad cow disease. Cats can be infected by a prion that causes a neurological disease, but only one case of this disease has been diagnosed in dogs. Controversy rages in the scientific, veterinary, and medical community over this disease so, at present, no definitive answer is available. Since parts of slaughtered animals, especially their brains and spinal cords, could be contaminated with prions, no such parts are permitted to be processed into the human food chain. But no such restrictions apply to the incorporation of such tissues into manufactured pet foods in the U.S.

AAFCO Nutrient Profiles

	Recommended Allowance	10 kg dog			
		Inactive	Weight Loss	Active	Weight Loss
Kcal/d	550	412	630	472	535
Kcal/100gm	350				400
	g/100 Kcal		g/day		
Protein	5.14	28.27	21	32.4	24
Carbohydrates	8.6	47.3	124	54.2	41
Fat	1.43	8	6	9	7
Fiber (Max)	1.4	7.7	6	8.8	7
	mg/100 Kcal		mg/d		
Calcium	170	935	700	1071	802
Phosphorous	140	770	577	882	661
Sodium	17	93.5	70	107.1	80
Potassium	170	935	700	1071	802
Chloride	26	143	107	163.8	123
Magnesium	11	60.5	45	69.3	52

NRC 2006

	Recommended Allowance	10 kg dog			
		Inactive	Weight Loss	Active	Weight Loss
Kcal/d	400	730	547		
Kcal/100gm					
	g/100 Kcal		g/day		
Protein	2.5	13	10	18.3	13.7
Carbohydrates	22.7	121	90.8	165.7	124.2
Fat	1.38	7	5.5	10.1	7.5
Fiber (Max)	0	0	0	0	
	mg/100 Kcal		mg/d		
Calcium	100	535	300	547.5	410.3
Phosphorous	75	401	300	547.5	410.3
Sodium	10	54	40	73	54.7
Potassium	1000	5350	4000	7300	5470
Chloride	15	80	60	109.5	82.1
Magnesium	15	80	60	109.5	82.1

Chapter 2

The Largest Pet Food Recall Ever

Pet Owners Get a Shocking Wake-Up Call

In March 2007, millions of concerned pet owners became aware of the massive recall by Menu Foods Income Fund of 60 million cans and packages of contaminated, poisonous cat and dog food. This one Canadian company produced over one billion containers of pet food in 2006. This compounded and processed food for dogs and cats was distributed to the major brand-name pet food companies and mega-stores for sale under many different labels, and appeared to be implicated in the development of acute kidney disease and even death in pets across the continent.

Menu Foods, after receiving many complaints about problems with its products, allegedly took three weeks to notify the United States Food and Drug Administration and occurred after running feed tests on some fifty cats and dogs, tests that resulted in the unnecessary suffering and deaths of even more animals.

Perhaps unrelated to all this and noted in the press as a horrible coincidence, the chief financial officer of Menu Foods sold about half of his stake in the company three weeks before the widespread pet food recall.

With this breach of consumer confidence, which pet food labels can be trusted? And how can the pet food industry itself be trusted?

The History

On March 19, 2007, the FDA notified the press that Menu Foods had performed tests on forty to fifty dogs and cats, ostensibly one week after receiving reports of pets dying from kidney failure. Seven of the test animals died. Cats were reported to be more severely affected than dogs. Apparently Iams, a pet food company for whom Menu Foods had been manufacturing foods, had contacted Menu Foods to report customer complaints of cats developing signs of kidney disease, and Menu Foods informed the FDA of problems on March 15. The company said it suspected that wheat gluten, a key ingredient in the formulation of pet food, could be the source of the problem, since the company had recently begun importing its wheat gluten from a new supplier in China.

This recall eventually involved about 100 different brand names and distributors, including major, well-known labels such as Iams, Eukanuba, Nutro, Hill's, Nutriplan, Royal Canin, Pet Pride, Natural Life vegetarian dog food, Your Pet, America's Choice-Preferred Pet, and Sunshine Mills, as well as store brands from such outlets as PetSmart, Publix, Winn-Dixie, Stop and Shop Companion, Price Chopper, Laura Lynn, Kmart, Longs Drug Stores Corp., Stater Bros. Markets, and Wal-Mart. The issue also encompassed a host of private labels of mainly canned (moist) cat and dog foods.

When coupled with the soon-to-follow recalls of brand names like Purina, Alpo, and Del Monte Pet Products, which are produced by pet food manufacturers that had bought the purportedly poisonous gluten themselves and did not contract with Menu Foods, the quantity of food recalled was in the hundreds of thousands of tons.

Pet Owners Learn the Limits of the FDA Powers

The shocking reality to pet owners is that the FDA has no mandatory authority to demand a pet food recall. All recalls are voluntary, upon written notification by the FDA. For example, in the recent past, upon the FDA's request, Iams stopped supplementing pet foods with cadmium (a toxic metallic element added to some prescription diets to increase the metabolism of overweight pets), and in early 2006, Royal Canin voluntarily recalled some of its prescription-only dog food that contained toxic levels of vitamin D_3, that is also, in high doses, used as a rat poison. But the truth is that there is no mandatory requirement for pet food manufacturers to inform the FDA in a timely fashion of risks and recalls nor is there any penalty for not doing so.

Rat Poison

On March 23, 2007, the New York State Department of Agriculture and Markets announced that it had found a chemical compound called aminopterin, sometimes used as rat poison, in wheat gluten imported from China. This was initially thought to be responsible for the suffering and deaths of an as yet unknown number of cats and dogs across North America.

A HUMAN ASPECT

After this recall hit the news, coauthor Michael Fox, who writes a syndicated column called "Animal Doctor," received letters from dog and cat owners thanking him for saving their animals' lives because the readers had been feeding their pets the homemade diet that Fox has been advocating for some years. Other letters documented the suffering and deaths of animals and their caregivers' disbelief, outrage, and financial and emotional losses. Many people reported veterinary bills from $3,000 to $6,000, and some, living on fixed incomes, said they had to put these expenses on credit cards and were paying exorbitant interest.

Veterinary toxicologists with the American Society for the Prevention of Cruelty to Animals and the American College of Internal Veterinary Medicine expressed concern that in addition to the aminopterin, there could be some other food contaminants that were sickening and killing pets. Experts were not convinced that the discovery of rat poison contamination was the end of the story.

The FDA could not find the rat poison in the samples it analyzed. However, a lab at the University of Guelph in Canada confirmed the presence of aminopterin. This chemical is also used in minute amounts as a DNA marker for crops that have been genetically engineered (known as genetically modified [GM] or transgenic crops) to be resistant to herbicides and to actually produce their own insecticides. This could mean that either the wheat gluten came from genetically engineered plants or that some other genetically engineered crop ingredient was in the contaminated pet food.

Herbicides

There is a possibility that glufosinate and glyphosate, herbicides that are applied repeatedly to crops across the U.S. and which are absorbed by crops that are genetically engineered to be resistant to these chemicals, (which, when sprayed on fields, kill only the weeds) could be part of the problem. These widely-used herbicides cause kidney damage and other health problems in laboratory-tested animals.

Genetically Modified Crops

Farmed animals are fed corn and other feeds from genetically engineered crops that produce their own insecticide called Bt. High levels of Bt in crops have poisoned sheep and made farmers ill. Since pet food labels don't show this, and the FDA does not insist on the labeling of human foods when they contain genetically modified ingredients, we have no way of knowing what we are really eating or feeding to our pets.

Although the U.S. has so far resisted the temptation of genetically engineering the staff of life—wheat, our daily bread—China has forged ahead, in collaboration with the UK Rothamsted Agricultural Research Center, to develop genetically modified varieties of wheat, as well as rice and other commodity crops.

Significantly, the UK Food Standards Agency reported on April 26, 2007, that an illegal shipment of rice protein concentrate from the genetically modified rice line, Bt63, had come from China via the Netherlands into the UK for incorporation into livestock feed and possibly pet foods. Unlike the laissez-faire attitude of the U.S. government toward genetically modified crops and foods, the UK has tight restrictions, and routinely monitors imported grains and other foods for evidence of having been genetically engineered, or containing ingredients from GM crops.

The agricultural biotechnology industry has convinced U.S. legislators that genetically engineered crops are safe and substantially equivalent to conventional varieties of food and animal feed crops. But the scientific evidence and documented animal safety tests point in the opposite direction (see Chapter 10). The U.S. government even attempted to have genetically engineered seeds and foods and municipal sewage sludge included in the National Organic Standards as acceptable.

Melamine

On March 30, 2007, the FDA reported finding a widely used compound called melamine, described as a chemical used in the manufacture of plastics and as a wood resin adhesive, in the wheat gluten. While the FDA officials told the media that melamine is fairly nontoxic, it claimed that the melamine was the probable cause of an undetermined number of cat and dog poisonings and deaths.

On April 6, the FDA Center for Veterinary Medicine director, Dr. Stephen Sundlof, told CNN that the melamine found in the contaminated wheat gluten from China could actually have been added as cheap filler. Melamine crystal is a urea-derived, synthetic nitrogen product that is used as a fertilizer.

How this melamine got into the gluten was still an open question in early April, and some toxicologists still doubted that this was the main cause of so many dogs and cats becoming sick and even dying from kidney failure.

It is possible that the presence of herbicides, such as glufosinate and glyphosate, in commercial pet foods could have made dogs and cats more susceptible to melamine and other urea-related chemical contaminants.

There also may be a connection between the melamine contamination and the melamine derivative cyromazine, which is used as a pesticide. It is not all that toxic and is actually fed to chickens to control fly larvae in their droppings.

Widely used as a spray, cyromazine is absorbed by plants and is then converted into melamine. When cyromazine is consumed by test animals, it is converted in their bodies, as in the plants, back to melamine.

On April 3, Associated Press named the U.S. importer of the poisonous pet food ingredient as ChemNutra of Las Vegas, reporting that the company had recalled 873 tons of wheat gluten that had been shipped to three pet food makers and a single distributor who in turn supplies the pet food industry. Close to 100 different brands' labels of cat and dog food were recalled.

Response to Pet Deaths

The FDA is both secretive and reassuring

This enormous pet food recall in North America mobilized the public and their elected representatives to take a closer look at how our food is produced and where it comes from.

The FDA's Stephen Sundlof told a Senate Appropriations Committee hearing on April 11, that the FDA had documented sixteen reported deaths and some 9,000 complaints of adverse reactions. This figure of sixteen deaths was curiously low since other Internet sources were reporting far more deaths and adverse reactions in pets.

Was the FDA deliberately downplaying the severity of this nationwide pet food poisoning scandal at this time? One major question had not yet been answered: Why had the imported wheat gluten, if it really was wheat gluten causing the problem, not also been bought by some U.S. human food manufacturers? Why was it only to be used in pet food?

The pet food institute forms a committee

Instead of compensating owners for their veterinary expenses incurred as a result of the tainted food, the pet food industry simply set up yet another expert committee. Holding up a full-page ad that the PFI had placed in major newspapers, Duane Ekedahl, head of the Pet Food Institute which represents the pet food industry, told the senators at the Appropriations Committee hearing that the institute had set up, as per the newspaper advertisement, a National Pet Food Commission. He asserted that, "Pet foods are perhaps the most-regulated product on market shelves." When challenged by Sen. Richard Durbin, representatives for the PFI and the American Association of Feed Control Officials (whose AAFCO labeling guidelines are standardized on most processed pet foods but offer no valid guarantee of quality or safety) became extremely defensive and contradicted themselves when it came to actual inspection and testing of ingredients. Sundlof cited that pet food processing facilities in the U.S. had a federal inspection rate frequency of only 30 percent for the previous three years. This was actually more than usual due to the mad cow disease issue.

The testimony of coauthor Elizabeth Hodgkins, a feline specialist in private practice in California who had served as director of technical affairs at Hill's Pet Food Nutrition, was the one clear voice of truth and reason. Her testimony (see Chapter 6) cut through all the crosstalk and obfuscation to document the pet food industry's lack of effective regulation, oversight, quality and safety controls, adequacy and accuracy of labeling, and verifiability of claimed nutritional value. She made it quite clear that cats in particular were becoming ill and dying well before the melamine scare because of some of the ingredients and formulations the U.S. pet food manufacturers were marketing to a trusting public. Far too many veterinarians still believe these foods are scientifically formulated, balanced, and in accord with the claims on the AAFCO standardized label, Hodgkins concluded.

Some elected officials respond

At hearings in the House of Representatives on April 24, Paul K. Henderson, Menu Food's CEO, pointed out that Menu's U.S. and Canadian plants must qualify to export food to Europe by passing annual inspections, and that, if a similar system had been set up for U.S. inspections of all foreign suppliers, it could have impacted Menu's situation.

We believe there is something to learn from this enlightened business arrangement enjoyed by the European pet food industry: Foreign suppliers to the U.S. should be inspected, certified, and accredited before transacting business within the U.S., just as they must do before selling to European businesses.

On May 9, the Senate passed a bill to amend the Food, Drug, and Cosmetic Act to require the Department of Health and Human Services to work to establish processing and ingredient standards for pet foods, updates to labeling standards, a system of surveillance, and a veterinary notification network. A separate Human and Pet Food Safety Act of 2007 introduced by Sen. Dick Durbin and Rep. Rosa DeLauro in their respective houses of Congress would give legal authority to HHS to order a mandatory recall and the responsibility to certify that the food safety programs of a foreign government or establishment are at least equivalent to U.S. programs before any imports into the U.S. are permitted.

More Recalls and More Discoveries

On April 18, 2007, because of melamine contamination, Wilbur-Ellis Co. of San Francisco, an importer of rice protein from China, voluntarily recalled all lots it had previously distributed to pet food manufacturers. It urged all manufacturers who had used this rice protein to recall any pet food that might still be on supermarket shelves.

Natural Balance was the first company to respond to this concern, recalling two of their dry foods for cats and dogs the same day.

This second recall epidemic spread as more pet food brands, such as Blue Buffalo dry kitten food, SmartPak Co. dry dog food, and several cat and dog dry foods manufactured by Royal Canin USA, were hastily recalled because of the contaminated rice protein. The rice protein was also found to contain a breakdown product of melamine, the more toxic cyanuric acid, a chemical used to chlorinate swimming pools. (Royal Canin also withdrew dog foods from the market in South Africa when corn gluten used in its manufacture there was found to be contaminated with melamine.)

The Wilber-Ellis Co. batch of rice protein also contaminated Chenango Valley Pet Foods products that went out under contract labels that included SmartPak, Lick Your Chops, and two catalog mail order brands, including Doctors Foster and Smith cat and dog foods.

On April 26, Diamond Pet Foods recalled three canned varieties of dog, puppy, and kitten food manufactured by American Nutrition, Inc. That same day, two more pet food recalls were announced by Costco Wholesale Corp. for some of its Kirkland Signature canned pet food, made also by American Nutrition, and Chenango Valley Pet Foods, who had used rice protein supplied by Wilbur-Ellis.

The most telling indictment of the pet food industry came from Blue Buffalo Co. in media releases issued by that company in April 2007. Blue Buffalo alleged product tampering by the manufacturer they had contracted with for some of their canned dog and cat foods and dog treats. They said the manufacturer had been adding rice protein [supplied by Wilbur-Ellis] without our knowledge or approval.

This press release revealed how dysfunctional the profit-driven pet food industry has become, where the bottom line is all about finding the lowest-cost ingredients to meet the quasi-scientific pet food industry nutrient values (where poultry feathers, hooves and horns can pass as animal protein), regardless of the source, true nutrient value, or possible inclusion of toxic contaminants.

The Chinese Connection

According to an Associated Press news release on April 20, 2007, the Chinese authorities had told the FDA that the wheat gluten was an industrial product not meant for pet food. In another release on April 26, AP reported the (Chinese) ministry said the contaminated vegetable protein managed to get through customs without inspection because it had not been declared for use in pet food. The FDA later admitted that because of staffing and funding limitations it was only able to inspect 1 percent of all imported food items from China.

The Washington Post, on April 30, quoted a Chinese food and feed processor as asserting that for several years urea was added as a cheap filler that would pass as protein under the crude ingredient tests done on food commodities. But when they mixed too much urea into livestock feed and made animals sick, they switched to melamine. So it is quite probable that this adulteration that has been going on for years, and importers of vegetable

WHY WHEAT GLUTEN?

Why import food commodities like wheat gluten from essentially unknown sources in the first place? Because it is cheaper than buying from North American sources.

But the bigger question is, why put wheat gluten and vegetable protein into food for carnivores like cats? By putting corn and other cereal byproducts with low-value vegetable protein into cat food in the quantities they do, U.S. pet food manufacturers do no less harm to America's pets than do the Chinese entrepreneurs that sell it to them. The same holds true with dogs. Many dogs often mirror the gluten-sensitivities (gluten is found in cereal grains and is the cause of celiac disease in humans) of their human companions with skin problems, allergies, colitis, etc. Many epileptic dogs have recovered when wheat gluten, other wheat products, and corn are removed from their diet.

protein from China have been putting U.S. consumers and their animal companions at risk for some time.

In May, The Beijing Morning Post announced that managers of two companies exporting contaminated wheat gluten and rice protein had been detained. The two companies were Xuzhou Anying Biological Technology Development Co. Ltd. and Binzhou Futian Biology Technology Co. Ltd. According to reporter Rick Weiss in the May 11, Post, when FDA inspectors arrived to investigate these two companies earlier that week, they found that the suspect facilities had been hastily closed down and cleaned up.

Later news reports indicated that the Xuzhou Anying facility had been razed to the ground by the manager, Mao Lijun, once he heard that the FDA was on its way. Apparently his industrial waste recycling plant had been spewing noxious fumes over an impoverished rural community, making people's eyes water. The fumes also killed nearby poplar trees. Appeals to local government officials since 2004 went unheeded.

On May 30, 2007, The New York Times reported that the

former commissioner of China's Food and Drug Administration, Zheng Xiaoyu, had been sentenced to death for his role in corruption and sales of counterfeit drugs and tainted and substandard food and drugs that had caused tens of thousands of people in China and around the world to become sick and even die.

Focusing on a Combination of Contaminants

On April 20, 2007, FDA scientists said they had identified three other contaminants in the urine and kidneys of animals sickened or killed after eating the recalled pet foods. These three chemicals were metabolized byproducts of melamine and more toxic than the parent chemical, namely amilorine, amiloride, and cyanuric acid. This kind of poisoning was suspected all along because melamine is not all that toxic at the levels found in contaminated pet foods.

Urea is an ammoniated waste product of the metabolic breakdown of proteins in humans and animals. Small amounts of urea-based chemicals, like melamine and cyanuric acid, fed to ruminants like cattle, goats, and sheep, does not harm them, but when given to dogs and cats it essentially reverses their metabolic cycle by feeding them the equivalent of their own body wastes. This results, in these pet foods-poisoned animals, in a buildup of urea in their blood, causing urea poisoning and kidney failure. This was confirmed subsequently by veterinary toxicologists at the University of California, Davis. Cats given various doses of either melamine or cyanuric acid survived, but cats given both chemicals developed kidney failure within twelve hours and had the same kind of kidney damage found in animals that had died from contaminated pet food.

Veterinary toxicologists faced yet another outbreak of pet food poisoning, this time from various brands of chicken jerky treats for dogs that Wal-Mart took off its shelves on July 26, 2007, after complaints from pet owners. These treats contained levels of melamine so low as to be considered non-toxic. No poisons were found by the FDA. But small dogs were particularly harmed, developing what is called acquired Fanconi syndrome in which there is necrosis (disintegration) of the kidney tubules. This progressive disease, which has a genetic origin in some breeds like the Basenji, causes a loss of bicarbonate in the urine, and calls for constant monitoring and appropriate alkali supplementation.

It is likely that a whole population of already kidney-challenged cats and dogs became the victims of this latest pet food tragedy because there were other contaminants in what they had been eating earlier in their lives that had already weakened their kidneys and other vital organs. Mercury in fish products for cats and herbicide residues in genetically modified foods that go into cat and dog foods could well have set the stage for thousands of kidney- and other vital organ-compromised animals to die.

Still More News Hits

On May 1, 2007, Reuters news service disclosed that the FDA was evaluating the authenticity of an estimated 4,000 reports of pet deaths that they had received from American households.

On May 2, a bill in the Senate was approved by a vote of 94-0 to require uniform federal standards for pet food ingredients and labeling, and to establish a registry of potentially contaminated food products to serve as an early warning system of problems with human or pet food. Companies were to be fined if they failed to report problems.

The Baltimore Sun gave more details on May 2 from the FDA, which said it had received 17,000 reports of cats and dogs becoming ill or dying, with as many as 1,950 cat and 2,200 dog deaths. Menu Foods expanded its pet food recall, because of concerns over cross-contamination at its manufacturing facility, to a total of 131 different brand labels that included 67 brands of cat food and 64 brands of dog food.

The actual number of animals that died will likely never be known, but on May 4, the Los Angeles Times quoted a source from the FDA that put the estimated number of dog and cat deaths at 8,500.

This news was joined by Cereal Byproducts Co., which announced on the same day that it was recalling contaminated rice protein it had imported from China and sold to three customers located in the Midwest. The names of these companies were not mentioned in the press release. Cereal Byproducts Co. stated it had

CONTAMINATED FOOD FED TO ANIMALS
DESTINED FOR HUMAN CONSUMPTION

About the same time as cats and dogs were dying in the pet foods poisoning scandal, a hog farm in California was under quarantine because, although the pigs were healthy, melamine was found in their urine. Their feed was suspect since Diamond Pet Foods' Lathrop, California, facility, whic produces Natural Balance pet food, had bought contaminated rice protein from China and had sold salvage pet food to the farm for pig feed. Curiously, in April 2007, a pink bag labeled melamine was found in a shipment of imported rice protein.

After pigs on farms in three states were quarantined after testing positive for melamine, on April 24, 2007, the FDA announced that it planned to expand testing of the animal food supply. Subsequent discovery of millions of broiler chickens in Indiana being fed contaminated rice protein raised the tenor of consumer concern and calls for a more effective FDA and food safety and security measures. Later, with little fanfare, the FDA approved the release of these chickens for human consumption.

On May 9, The Washington Post reported that an untold number of farm-raised fish were being fed melamine-contaminated wheat flour that had been imported from China by a Canadian fish food processor.

On May 31, The New York Times reported that FDA officials had announced that a manufacturing plant in Toledo, Ohio, a subsidiary of Tembec BTLSR, a Canadian forest products company, was using melamine to make binding agents for the manufacture of pelletized fish and shrimp food and livestock feed being exported abroad and distributed in the U.S.

"proactively" notified its customers, and had implemented its own voluntary recall of the contaminated products on or about April 19, 2007.

FDA to Close Labs

Adding insult to injury, specifically to America's pets because of the evident holes in the FDA and other government agencies' effectiveness in meeting their public service responsibilities, the FDA announced plans to close down seven of its thirteen field laboratories. In a May 3 McClatchy Newspapers article, Terry Pugh, reporting this insanity, stressed that these field labs inspect and analyze food and drugs destined for human and animal use, as well as medical devices and other health products.

At a media briefing on May 8, Dr. David Acheson, assistant commissioner for food protection with the FDA, surprised everyone by claiming that there never was any wheat gluten or rice protein in the pet foods. He said it had been wheat flour spiked with melamine and related compounds that had been actually mislabeled as wheat gluten and rice protein by Chinese exporters. As for the aminopterin (the rat poison and possible genetic marker) that the FDA and Cornell University labs were unable to confirm in the samples they tested, Dr. Dan Rice, director of the New York State Food Laboratory Division, contended that this was most probably due to the nature of this chemical that breaks down quickly if food samples are not shielded from light.

Also on May 8, the Times reported that cyanuric acid (the substance toxicologists contend has increased toxicity when combined in an animal's body with melamine) is indeed routinely put into livestock feed in China to artificially boost the nitrogen content—a cheap source of protein for ruminant animals like cattle—and thus profits.

Pet food recalls continued, and Castor and Pollux Pet Works issued a recall on four canned foods for cats on May 11. Royal Canin USA announced the recalls of eight Sensible Choice dog food products and seven Kasco dry dog and cat food products on May 14. That these recalls came weeks after the initial flurry of pet food recalls makes one wonder about the internal organization and management structure of these companies. The gradual

A PREVIOUS PET FOOD CATASTROPHE

USA Today reported on March 10, 2008, that Dr. Cathy Brow, a specialist in kidney disease at Georgia's Athens Veterinary Diagnostic Laboratory, insightfully got preserved samples of kidneys from pets that died in the massive pet food poisoning in Asia in 2004. She found the same insoluble crystals in the kidney samples as were being reported in the U.S. pet food poisoning.

Hundreds, and possibly thousands, of cats and dogs died from consuming contaminated Pedigree dog foods and Whiskas cat food manufactured in Thailand by Mars Inc.

This company apparently already knew about this linkage between the two outbreaks and informed the FDA in March 2007, but failed to also inform the American Veterinary Medical Association, the American Association of Veterinary Laboratory Diagnosticians, the Pet Food Institute, and the American Feed Control Officials.

increase in recalls over such a protracted period shows a shameful lassitude on the part of all responsible parties.

Interestingly, reporter Lisa Wade McCormick in a May 15 article for Consumer Affairs.Com wrote, "Since March, eighteen companies have recalled more than 5,600 pet food products because they contained imported and mislabeled ingredients tainted with melamine-related derivatives."

If valid, this number of products recalled far exceeds the FDA public list that, by May 31, showed 458 varieties of cat food and 685 varieties of dog food that had been recalled. (Several ferret and tropical fish food recalls were also mentioned.)

Two Months into the Pet Food Recall

Reporter Rick Weiss' article in the Post on May 20 titled "Tainted Chinese Imports Common; In Four Months FDA Refuses 298 Shipments," put the pet food debacle into the larger arena where the problem began and where solutions may lie.

U.S. pet and human food producers look for the lowest food ingredient prices across the world market. Knowing this, Jin Zemin, manager of Shanghai Kaijin Bio-Tech, a Chinese company that specializes in wheat gluten, was quoted in USA Today as saying U.S. importers want cheap prices, but that can come with a cost.

While pet owners in Europe were being reassured by the European Pet Food Industry Federation that they had adequate mechanisms in place to assure quality and safety standards of ingredients, in the light of the situation in China, one can find little reassurance in the words of a Pet Food Manufacturers Association spokesperson that there are some ingredients that can only be sourced from China. An example of this is certain amino acids. To not include such ingredients would have a detrimental effect on the nutritional quality of the pet food.

That these and other nutrients need to be added to processed pet foods raises a host of other issues that we addressed in Chapter 1 and will revisit in Chapter 3.

Still More

Certainly 2007 was a bad year for the U.S.-based multinational pet food industry. As pet foods continued to be tested for contaminants, the discovery of potentially toxic levels of acetaminophen (used as a pain reliever and anti-inflammatory in humans) in several brands of cat and dog food produced by EperTox labs in Deer Park, Texas, sparked a new federal investigation. Acetaminophen is especially toxic to cats. As of this writing, the source of this contaminant has not been determined, but it is most likely due to cross-contamination at a chemical manufacturing plant marketing other drugs and food supplements and additives.

Mars Petcare issued recalls for two dry dog food products contaminated with salmonella bacteria. The United States Centers for Disease Control investigated this as a likely source of salmonella food poisoning in several states, especially in infants getting into the dog's food bowl.

Cat and dog foods containing poultry ingredients contaminated with salmonella and listeria were recalled by Bravo pet food company, and Castleberry recalled some Natural Balance dog foods because of possible botulism contamination. A salmonella-contaminated cat vitamin supplement was recalled by the Hartz Mountain Corp.

Vested Interests

There are many vested interests that would like to see this poisoned pet food pandemic forgotten because it exposes the unhealthful nature of industrial food production, processing, and marketing that harms people and their animal companions, and wreaks havoc on wildlife and our natural environment as a whole. Mercury, lead, arsenic, cadmium, dioxins, and thousands of other industrial pollutants, including highly toxic petrochemicals, fertilizers, herbicides, fungicides, and insecticides—used, ironically, in the production and preservation of food—now contaminate our drinking water and even the milk of human, polar bear, whale, and elephant mothers.

This morass of chemicals leads to the untimely death, often after prolonged suffering, of our loved ones, including our animal companions. This unacceptable situation will continue as long as there is public apathy and indifference rather than outrage and political action.

Will Class Action Lawsuits Be Part of the Solution?

There was a surge of class action suits seeking compensation for damages and emotional distress from pet food companies whose products resulted in the suffering and death of cats and dogs. Judges will have to deal with the fact that these animals are not simply property. As Pet Food Institute's Duane Ekedahl stated at the Senate Appropriations Committee hearings, cats and dogs are not just pets. They are family. Their emotional, social, psychological, and well-documented medical value to their human guardians are far beyond their replacement cost as a possession.

A federal multi-district litigation panel met in Las Vegas at the end of May 2007 to determine in which court the more than 800 cases against Menu Foods will be heard.

While financial compensation can never be enough for the loss of a beloved pet, class action suits can motivate food companies to be more vigilant, as per Diamond Pet Food's agreement to a $3.1 million settlement in January 2008 over the deaths of dozens of dogs from aflatoxin mold poisoning that contaminated the corn in their manufactured pet foods in late 2005.

The final outcome of more than 100 lawsuits on behalf of the thousands of aggrieved pet owners whose cats and dogs were poisoned and even killed after eating the contaminated pet food in this 2007 pet food industry debacle, were settled with unprecedented speed in April 2008. Owners could share a proposed $32 million settlement that would cover out-of-pocket expenses, including veterinary bills, and add a little extra for undocumented expenses. Pet owners could receive up to $900 for reasonable economic damages submitted without documentation. This was seen by many as emotional damages compensation, since loss of wages could come from being emotionally devastated and unable to work.

Contaminated Pet Food Case Ends in Fine, Probation

A Nevada couple who imported more than 800 metric tons of wheat gluten from China which was contaminated deliberately with melamime and cyanuric acid and killed an estimated 1,950 cats and 2,200 dogs in the US were sentenced in Kansas City on February 05, 2010.

Stephen and Sally Miller of Las Vegas and their company, ChemNutra, Inc., were fined $35,000 and placed on probation for three years and barred from importing pet food ingredients. *Kansas City Star* reporter Sara Shepherd writes:

"U.S. Magistrate Judge John T. Maughmer said he read a stack of letters, inches tall, from affected pet owners. Evidence doesn't indicate that the Millers knowingly imported something they knew would kill animals, the judge said. But they did not exercise due diligence to ensure their product was safe, he said. 'There was much loss, much heartbreak, much damage that was done as a consequence of this case...and you have to bear responsibility," Maughmer told the couple. In light of a $24 million settlement in a civil lawsuit related to the tainted food, the judge ordered no further restitution for pet owners."

Apparently, Suzhou Textiles, an export broker, mislabeled these 800 metric tons of tainted wheat gluten manufactured by Xuzhou to avoid inspection in China. Suzhou then did not properly declare the contaminated product it shipped to the U.S. as a material to be used in food, the indictment said. According to the indictment, Chem-Nutra picked up the melamine-tainted product at a port of entry in Kansas City, then sold it to makers of various brands of pet foods. The indictment alleges that Xuzhou added the melamine to artificially boost the protein content of the gluten to meet the requirements specified in Suzhou's contract with ChemNutra.

Should We Be Thankful?

Perhaps, when all the numbers are in and the mortalities and morbidity rates of cats and dogs more fully collated, the West should thank China for exposing (tragically as it was through the suffering and deaths of uncounted numbers of beloved animal companions) that our global food supply, in terms of quality, safety, and healthfulness is critically dysfunctional. Certainly, the U.S. is no better than China or any other country when money rules and ignorance and indifference prevail. Every government should be called to address the deeper layers of the problem, from corruption to lack of standards and ineffective oversight. The largest pet food recall so far is likely the tip of the iceberg. To prevent the occurrence of future recalls, appropriate government action, multilaterally, is our best hope.

Bottom of the Human Food Chain

Long ago, dogs scavenged and cleared up our garbage. They survived, and it was all organic anyway and still they do today, but now at their own risk because the human garbage and human food-industry byproducts recycled into pet foods are no longer organic. As for the new generation designer and premium brands of highly advertised (and highly processed) dry dog and cat foods, just read the labels and you are still likely to find that the bulk of the ingredients is made up of cereal byproducts, and the main protein source is cheap vegetable and animal protein meal. These dietary formulations are based on clinically unsound and scientifically dubious nutritional analyses and determinations

IT'S NOT JUST FOOD, IT'S DRUGS, TOO

Regrettably, in the middle of this massive pet food recall, another issue that involved the documented deaths of some 500 dogs and much animal suffering did not get the press attention that it deserved. This involved the FDA and its handling of one of its staff, veterinarian Victoria "Tory" Hampshire, who was unjustifiably transferred because of it. The issue was over Hampshire's initiative to get a recall on a veterinary prescription drug, ProHeart 6, that pharmaceutical multinational Wyeth, through its veterinary subsidiary Fort Dodge, wanted kept on the market in spite of Hampshire's documented concerns. This product, moxidectin, prescribed to control heartworms, is still being marketed in Canada and is registered in eight other international markets, and may soon regain FDA approval for use in the U.S.

that are passed off as sound nutritional science endorsed by veterinarians, breeders, and celebrities.

Many premium-labeled pet foods were just as poisonous as cheaper brands and varieties in this latest recall. This is no less unethical than Chinese merchants putting urea-derived melamine into wheat flour and marketing it as high-protein wheat gluten for export and domestic use. The current ingredient labeling on most pet foods uses some industry terminology that is unintelligible to anyone without insider knowledge. At best, this is misleading to the average pet owner who must rely on and trust, and, at worst, it borders on deception. To make matters worse, there is no reference as to country of origin of any of the ingredients.

So what can we do as consumers? Grow our own food, support our local organic farmers markets, eat foods in-season, cook from scratch, and when we outsource, trust the USDA's organic-certified label. We can support non-government organizations that monitor and oppose continued attempts by agribusiness to undermine the National Organic Standards. You can learn about these organizations in publications like ACRES, USA's sustainable agriculture books. More insights on this will be given in Chapter 10.

Chapter 3

Pet Foods: A Veterinary and Ethical Evaluation

The quality and safety of the food people feed their families is of increasing concern as consumers are becoming more aware of the importance of good nutrition to health, vitality, disease resistance, and longevity. Since dogs and cats are part of the family, it is a natural extension of consumer concern about human food quality and safety for people to become concerned also about the quality and safety of commercial pet foods. Good nutrition is one of the cornerstones of human and animal health. Diet and lifestyle for both people and their companion animals influence health and longevity.

But the mere convenience of commercial pet foods is no valid reason for informed consumers to continue to feed them to their pets in all good conscience.

Correcting dietary excesses, nutrient imbalances and deficiencies, and various food contaminants and adulterants is a task that no government can hope to achieve. This task is the responsibility of us all, from farmer and rancher, food processor and retailer, to human and animal health care providers, nutrition educators, and consumers alike.

This current debacle of the commercial processed pet food industry puts us all on notice. Better quality controls, oversight, and testing are called for, but one must be realistic. There have been recent massive recalls of human food, including ground beef, poultry, onions, spinach and tomatoes. Costs aside, no system of mass production can be completely safe. The recycling of human food industry byproducts, and products considered unfit for human consumption, into livestock feed and processed pet food presents a monumental risk-management challenge.

Food Safety and Quality Test Limitations

Long-term scientific studies of various feed formulations and pet food ingredients on cats and dogs of different ages, during pregnancy and lactation, and for animals of various breeds, are not economically realistic. Because the scientific method cannot be applied cost-effectively to rigorously determine processed pet food quality and safety, veterinarians have adopted the clinical method. This pragmatic approach entails changing or supplementing pets' regular commercial diet until symptoms of suspected diet-related problems are resolved. Alternatively, pets are put on specially formulated prescription diets. (See Chapters 5 and 8.)

But as veterinarians, we want to do more than just wait for problems to happen to companion animals. The best medicine, whenever possible, is always prevention. This principle applies to pet nutrition and diet-related disorders. Logically, except for cats and dogs with inherited or acquired diet-related health problems, a natural diet of various whole foods appropriate for the species makes biological sense. Scientific studies and often cruel animal tests are surely not needed when appropriate whole foods are fed to our pets.

Ethically-questionable invasive procedures are sometimes used in determining the digestibility of commercial pet food ingredients—like inserting a tube through a dog's flank into the intestines to draw out samples of food to evaluate digestibility—because instead of whole foods with known digestibility, commercial pet foods contain highly processed human food industry byproducts as main ingredients, along with various synthetic additives, supplements, and preservatives. But even if noninvasive scientific studies and clinical trials were set up, these pet foods would still not provide adequate nutrition as the animals are not physiologically adapted to these biologically novel, if not dangerous, ingredients. Low-cost, low-nutrition fillers in pet food—ingredients like corn starch, wheat bran, and beet pulp—are the antithesis of whole, unmodified, and natural raw and cooked foods.

Food Industry Sources of Pet Food Ingredients

Many conventionally raised crops are from artificially fertilized soils that are deficient in essential nutrients. These deficiencies, along with various herbicide, insecticide, and fungicide chemical residues—and not infrequently toxic molds (like afla-toxin)—are in the foods we eat and feed to our animals. Also, an increasing numbers of crops are genetically engineered, many varieties of which produce their own pesticides and may undergo unpredictable mutations altering nutritive value and safety, caus-ing further harm to consumers, as shown in several animal toxicity studies (see Chapter 10 and Appendix B).

Reducing reliance upon chemicals and genetic engineering coupled with the broad adaptation of organic farming practices that create healthy soils and crops is becoming more and more urgent, and is something consumers and veterinarians should be pushing for.

We all need to be concerned about contaminants—bacte-rial, drug, agrichemical, and other—the low nutritional value, and the variable quality from batch to batch of rendered animal parts from slaughterhouses. Viral and prion contaminants can be very dangerous, as can be seen with the devastating consequences of the mad cow disease epidemic (bovine spongiform encepha-lopathy) that began in the U.K. This epidemic was attributed to prion-contaminated offal put into livestock feed and pet and zoo animal foods, which caused several cats and zoo animals and one dog to develop this disease.

Veterinarian David Jaggar, a well-known holistic animal doc-tor, shared the following account with us of his earlier professional experience working in slaughterhouses.

> "Having worked in U.S. slaughterhouses, I can attest that the designation 'beef' could mean it is the bruised trimmings from a fractured leg or a calf fetus, and the liver could be one parasit-ized by liver fluke, if not so extensive as to make the whole liver cirrhotic. The beef could be from an animal with leukemia, etc. Some of the criteria are written for when slaughtered animals must be condemned for both human and animal consumption, but outside those limits, much is left to the lay and veterinary meat inspectors in a slaughterhouse as to what else is kept out of animal consump-tion. Management places considerable pressure on the inspectors to pass as much of the human consumption condemned material as is possible for nonhuman animal consumption."

The U.S. National Renderers Association estimates that around 1.56 billion pounds of dead stock—so-called 4-D meat from animals who are dead, dying, debilitated or diseased—are rendered every year. According to Rendering Magazine, an industry periodical, rendering…removes the need to dispose of byproducts in landfills or by other methods that might pose potential health risks or strain existing landfill space. The 47 billion pounds of raw material processed by the rendering industry each year would make a truck convoy four lanes wide from Los Angeles, California, to New York City, New York. What else can the livestock industry do with all this offal, which is too much to be put into landfills or incinerated? Why not profit from recycling it into pet food and farm animal feed? This is a question that veterinarians and pet owners must address and not leave to people seeking maximum profit with minimum effort and expenditure.

This problematic situation, a consequence of far too many farm animals being raised for human consumption, is now being questioned by ecologists, agricultural economists, humane and consumer advocates, and public health authorities. Many consumers are also questioning the ethics of supporting the continuation of cruel, intensive methods of livestock production.

Even though some pet food manufacturers are now marketing premium foods with fewer byproducts and artificial preservatives, the sources of animal ingredients in these foods as well—still primarily from factory farms and from a seafood industry that continues to harm dolphins, other marine life, and ocean ecosystems from overfishing—are justly questionable.

One Food Not for All

Until recently, most dog and cat owners believed that one kind of cat or dog food was good for all breeds and sizes and that feeding human food and table scraps was taboo because it could upset the balance of scientifically formulated ingredients. Now, all of this is changing, thanks to advances in animal nutrition and the often remarkable health improvements that veterinarians have reported in their animal patients when taken off manufactured pet foods and put on whole food diets, which are often homemade.

(It is ironic that many cats and dogs with food allergies, skin problems, diarrhea, and colitis—problems that might never have been encountered if they had been fed an unprocessed diet of whole foods from the start—are put on costly hypoallergenic or limited antigen commercial diets.)

Veterinarians W. Jean Dodds and S. Donohue have done some landmark studies of breed differences in nutritional requirements, showing how nutrition plays a significant role in disease and disease prevention, e.g., alkaline diets for miniature schnauzers with kidney or bladder calcium oxalate stones; vitamin A (in the form of etretinate) supplements for cocker spaniels and other breeds with seborrhea, an extremely distressing greasy-skin disease; wheat-free diets for Irish setters with wheat-sensitive enteropathy, a severe inflammatory bowel disease. For animals with impaired immune systems, vitamin B_6 (pyridoxine), vitamin E, zinc, selenium and linoleic acid are helpful supplements.

Dodds reports that dogs genetically prone to thyroid and other autoimmune diseases show generalized improvements when fed premium cereal-based diets preserved naturally with vitamins C and E, combined with fresh, home-cooked vegetables with herbs, low-fat dairy products and meats such as lamb, chicken, and turkey.

The science of nutrition is progressing significantly thanks to recent advances in the genetics of disease. So-called nutritional genomics points to individual and breed differences in nutrient requirements, and in the appropriate use of nutraceutical supplements in treating sick animals with genetically associated diseases such as diabetes mellitus, heart disease, chronic kidney disease, and various forms of cancer. Indeed, nutrients can have an epigenetic effect, either accentuating or modulating various gene expressions and processes. This means that the mother's diet can affect the development of her offspring's physiology, metabolism, even stress and disease resistance, for better or for worse.

High carbohydrate consumption and overfeeding lead to obesity and diabetes. Puppies, especially of those breeds that are prone to obesity (e.g., labradors, beagles, basset hounds, dachshunds, cocker spaniels, and Shetland sheepdogs), should be on a restricted calorie diet until ten months of age in order to avoid developing hip dysplasia and other obesity-related health problems later in life.

Adding Supplements Is Risky

When whole foods in the right proportions are not used in formulating commercial diets for dogs and cats, the addition of nutrient supplements is necessary, but poses a potential risk. For example, in 2000, Iams pet food company recalled 248,000 pounds of dry dog food because excessive quantities of the amino acid DL-methionine had been put into the manufactured product. This company was subsequently requested by the FDA to recall prescription diet dog food with the added supplement of chromium, which was intended to help control weight by increasing dogs' metabolism. In 2006, Waltham's Royal Canin had to recall several types of dog food because excessive, harmful quantities of vitamin D_3 had been added.

Dodds cites several studies that give a clearer understanding of the possible cause of hypothyroidism in dogs. Cereal grains grown in iodine-deficient soils and in soils deficient in selenium (an essential trace mineral that plays a role in thyroid gland function) may not provide dogs (and humans too) with sufficient iodine and selenium. Synthetic antioxidants in pet foods, the safety of which has been long proclaimed by manufacturers, may contribute to the genesis of thyroid disease in dogs because they can change the digestive system's ability to absorb selenium, as well as vitamins A and E's so-called bioavailability.

A deficiency in dietary phosphate can result in pica (eating dirt) or depraved appetite. This may be the reason for some dogs to engage in coprophagia (eating their own stools). Excess calcium in the diet can cause phosphate deficiency. Other dietary deficiencies, however, may also play a role in the genesis of coprophagia and pica. Pica is a common sign of iron-deficiency anemia in dogs.

A high salt (sodium chloride) content in pet foods can cause hypertension and result in increased kidney and heart disease susceptibility. Chronic high protein consumption in dogs is to be avoided because feeding less protein and more fats and carbohydrates may help increase longevity by slowing kidney degeneration (glomerulosclerosis).

The form of various nutrients indicated on the pet food label may be misleading to purchasers. For example, indicating the presence and amount of various minerals is all very well, but if these minerals are not chelated organic minerals, they will not be assimilated well. Food quality also varies depending on how it was commercially processed and stored. Even purportedly high-quality premium diets have been found to have fatal consequences for pets, like taurine deficiency. Lack of taurine, an essential amino acid, can result in enlarged and weakened hearts (cardiomyopathy) and blindness in cats.

Even though this problem was subsequently corrected by manufacturers, scientists do not yet know everything necessary about the nutritional requirements of pets being fed entirely processed foods. This is why more veterinarians now recommend various high-quality natural commercial diets (containing few, if any, processed food industry byproducts, and supplements/additives) and supplementation with fresh food in proper balance.

It has been long known that food processing lowers the nutritional value of food. Cooking, for example, improves the digestibility of cereals in commercial pet foods, but can destroy certain vitamins and enzymes and denature proteins, lowering or eliminating essential amino acids. Hence, the increasing interest by human and veterinary nutritionists in the benefits of raw foods and advocacy of home-cooked foods (see recipes in Appendix A).

Another advantage of home-cooked pet food—besides the fact that you know exactly what is in it—is the fact that much of the animal protein and fat in manufactured pet foods is subjected to high-temperature cooking not once but twice: first during the rendering process (at 100 to 120 degrees centigrade) and then again during the preparation of ingredients for canned, semi-moist, and dry pet food products. Heating denatures animal protein, making it less digestible, and also lowers its nutritional value by destroying various amino acids like tyrosine and other essential nutrients, such as vitamins and essential fatty acids. Cooking may also convert proteins in meat to DNA-damaging compounds that can play a role in cancer and other health problems.

Many pet foods that contain a mixture of cereal grains, soybean meal, and animal byproducts are deficient in several amino acids, notably methionine, arginine, threonene, and leucine. Cereals are high in phytases, allelochemicals that interfere with calcium uptake and lead to calcium deficiency diseases. Cereals often form the bulk of commercial pet foods, which, for cats and dogs, can mean obesity, diabetes, arthritis, and food allergies; cystitis in cats and seizures or epilepsy in dogs. Obesity is a common problem in cats, in particular, when they are allowed free access to a dry food dispenser.

Essential Fatty Acids

Dry pet foods are generally deficient in essential fatty acids. Dogs and cats on dry commercial foods often develop symptoms of essential fatty acid deficiencies, notably a dull coat, scaly skin, and susceptibility to skin and ear infections. Painful chronic inflammatory conditions like arthritis and gingivitis may be aggravated by such deficiencies. This serious deficiency in dry, manufactured pet foods has been recently addressed by most pet food manufacturers with additives and supplements touted as beneficial on the label. Why the long delay in rectifying this serious essential fatty acid deficiency problem while all along falsely claiming that the food was complete and scientifically formulated and balanced before this deficiency was acknowledged? It was well known in the UK over fifty years ago that a little flaxseed oil in the dog's food every day would make the dog's coat shine.

For young animals, a deficiency in essential fatty acids means slowed growth. With severe deficiencies, brain development and I.Q. can be impaired. Clinical studies have shown that old dogs improve physically and mentally when their diets are supplemented with a quality vegetable oil.

Vegetable oils only provide the omega-6 fatty acids linoleic and linolenic, but not arachidonic acid. Dogs, but not cats, can synthesize arachidonic acid from linoleic acid. Cats suffering from essential fatty acid deficiency, often manifested as chronic skin, joint, and other inflammatory conditions, must be given fish oil since it contains high levels of arachidonic acid.

With the exception of arachidonic acid, these vital nutrients are far more concentrated in vegetable oils than in animal fat, which too often, has excess omega-6 that can aggravate inflammatory conditions. Flaxseed oil is an excellent source of a wide spectrum of both omega-6 and omega-3 fatty acids in an optimally balanced ratio. Omega-3 fatty acids have recently been found to help alleviate some skin conditions and inflammatory disorders, notably chronic arthritis and inflammatory bowel disease in dogs.

Daily supplements of nutraceuticals like chondroitin, glucosamine, MSM, and turmeric also help dogs and cats suffering from arthritis, a very common malady in pets today. Vegetable oils may also help prevent and alleviate chronic renal failure in animals with kidney disease. Fish oil has been found to be more effective than flaxseed oil in helping dogs with arthritis, and may help with other chronic inflammatory diseases, especially gingivitis and related dental problems in cats and dogs that will not be cured by dental chew-sticks and other such commercial gimmicks.

With lower levels of essential fatty acids in factory farm-derived (and not USDA Certified Organic) animal produce, both consumers and their pets need to take supplements high in omega-3 fatty acids.

Synthetic Antioxidants

Dodds says, it is tempting to speculate that the rising incidence of leukemia, lymphomas, hemangiosarcomas, and chronic immunosuppressive disorders among companion animals is due at least partially to the widespread use of chemical antioxidants and other additives in commercial pet foods used as preservatives, especially to stop fats from turning rancid. Pet owners are advised, therefore, to avoid commercial foods and treats containing synthetic antioxidants like BHA, BHT, propyl gallate, and ethoxyquin. These synthetic chemicals can result in imbalances of essential vitamins and minerals when they disrupt the body's natural antioxidant system, and interfere with hormone synthesis. Toy breeds of dogs may be especially at risk because they eat proportionately more food for their size than larger breeds.

Ethoxyquin, a known carcinogen, was routinely used by pet food manufacturers until recently, but may still be added to tallow by renderers to prevent spoilage. Vitamin E or alpha tocopherols are now used as antioxidants by most pet food manufacturers, and some are also including extract of rosemary for this same purpose of preventing fats from going rancid.

More Potentially-Dangerous Additives

A variety of other additives are included in various pet foods to stop bacterial spoilage and to maintain desired color, texture, and flavor.

- Antimicrobials and antifungals in soft moist foods include potassium sorbate, sodium nitrite, and phosphoric, citric and other acids.
- Flavor and palatability enhancers include phosphoric acid and enzyme "digests" of poultry, liver, beef, and fish sprayed onto dry foods. Monosodium glutamate (MSG) is widely used, often under the term of "natural flavor enhancer," and can cause seizures, and possibly increased aggression in dogs.
- Coloring agents include azo (derived from coal tar) and non-azo dyes and natural coloring from carotenoids, even marigolds, and iron oxide.
- Color stabilizers include bisulfites, nitrites and ascorbates.
- Humectants, used to retain moisture, like sugar/sucrose, corn syrup, sorbitol and molasses; antimicrobial preservatives like propionic, sorbic and phosphoric acids, sodium nitrite, sodium and calcium propionate and potassium sorbate.
- Natural coloring agents like iron oxide and caramel, and synthetic coloring agents like coal tar-derived azo dyes such as Yellow 5, Red 40, Yellow 6, and Blue 2. Red 2G food coloring has been identified by the European Food Standards Authority as a carcinogen, and other coal tar- and petrochemical-derived azo dyes used as food (and beverage) coloring agents are now being

re-evaluated. The natural coloring agent annatto, from the tropical achiote tree, widely used in coloring cheese and other foods, can cause seizures in dogs.

- Emulsifying agents used as stabilizers and thickeners to make gravy, such as seaweed, seed, and microbial gums, gums from trees, and chemically modified plant cellulose like citrus pectin, xanthan, guar gum, and carrageenan.
- Natural fiber like beet pulp, and miscellaneous additives like polyphosphates that help retain natural moisture, condition and texture of manufactured pet foods.

The marketer's touting chicken byproduct meal as a "source of chondroitin and glucosamine that's good for pets' joints" in reality means that much of this ingredient is probably of low protein value because it contains a lot of cartilage and bone from the remains of ground-up chicken parts not considered fit for human consumption.

In semi-moist foods, humectants are added to maintain a soft texture and to prevent bacterial and fungal spoilage. Propylene glycol was widely used for this purpose until it was found to cause blood abnormalities. Instead, sorbitol, sucrose, molasses, corn syrups, and salt are used. Semi-moist foods are the ultimate junk food for pets.

The safety and toxicity of these various pet food additives cannot be accurately determined, not only because of individual differences in animals, but because of other chemical contaminants already present in certain ingredients and food and beverage industry byproducts not considered fit for human consumption. The main problem lies in the potential increase in toxicity when two or more artificial ingredients are present, and when these ingredients are broken down in the process of digestion.

Other Manufactured Pet Food Problems

While high temperature processing may destroy most harmful bacteria, cooking will not destroy bacterial endotoxins and fungal aflatoxins, which are frequent contaminants of animal parts and livestock feed-grade cereals.

Canned foods, with a 75 percent water content, are generally more palatable and digestible than dry foods. Chunks of artificially colored and textured soy protein (TVP) and wheat gluten that look like pieces of meat or liver, are easily mistaken by caregivers for the real thing, which is the manufacturer's intent. Soy protein is nonetheless quite nutritious for dogs, although it can cause bloating and allergic reactions in some. The high estrogen content of soy products calls for caution: all things in moderation for the more omnivorous dog and his master.

But cats, being obligatory carnivores, should have all their protein and fat requirements from animal sources only, ideally organic, humane, and sustainably produced. Such biologically irregular and wholly inappropriate ingredients of plant origin in cats' diets, like soy protein and wheat and rice gluten, play a major role in many cat health problems as detailed in chapters 7 and 9. Cats are especially sensitive to toxic ingredients in their food, water, and physical/home environment, many contaminants of which disrupt the endocrine system and immune system. This has been documented in a review of this endocrine-immune disruption syndrome in two books by coauthor Fox: *Cat Body, Cat Mind* and *Dog Body, Dog Mind.* Even the bisphenol-containing liners of pop-top cat food cans have been implicated in this syndrome, and reported as a significant factor in the high incidence of hyperthyroidism in cats, along with in-home exposure to fire-retardant chemicals.

Food Addiction

Several years ago, the pet food industry approached Fox for advice on animal behavior and psychology studies of food preference and food imprinting. He had published studies on olfactory (odor) imprinting in pups and great interest was evident in discussion of food aversion, anorexia, and especially, food imprinting and addiction. Since this consultation some thirty years ago, it is quite probable that research has been done on various food ingredients and synthetic additives that enhance palatability. These ingredients may be proprietary information and are not indicated on the pet food label of contents, or they may be listed without explanation, like natural flavor, animal digest, or artificial flavor.

Getting a dog or cat addicted at an early age to a particular brand, like a puppy or kitten food that contains appetite-enhancing, addictive additives, and including these same additives in dry and canned diets for adult animals, makes good marketing sense. But food addiction could be very detrimental to an animals' long-term health if they are constantly craving food, if the manufactured formula does not provide optimal nutrition, and if the animals refuse to eat other kinds of more healthful food. This is especially problematic with cats that, in particular, become addicted to dry food and refuse all else.

Unfortunately, many pet owners equate enthusiastic acceptance of a food as evidence of its nutritional value. Even the respectedConsumer Reports, in its controversial story on pet food, relied on taste tests done with employees' own pets as one criteria of a food's value. This, of course, is as silly as relying on a three-year-old child's nutritional sense to select a healthy treat among candy, ice cream, and carrots. Widely criticized by both veterinarians and the pet food industry for its failure to address issues such as digestibility, bioavailability, optimal nutrition, and ingredient quality, this article was seen by many as causing immeasurable harm to U.S. pets by promoting poor quality pet food.

Animals normally exercise what is called nutritional wisdom over their choice when they are provided with natural and whole foods. Such instinctual wisdom may be disrupted by odor and flavor enhancers added to manufactured pet foods resulting in animals preferring to eat processed foods over natural foods. This can give pet caregivers the false impression that commercial pet foods must be better than home-prepared diets because their animals show a preference for processed foods.

Bioethical Considerations

There are several ethical areas of concern that need to be considered in determining the kind and quality of food that people should give to their feline and canine companions. The term bioethics rather than ethics is preferable because ethics has more to do with how we behave toward each other, while bioethics has a broader scope, dealing with the ethical and moral implications of new biological advances and genetic research.

Fox defined bioethics in his book Eating With Conscience: The Bioethics of Food as the extension of ethical issues and concerns from the immediate human community into the broader biological dimension of our relations with and duties toward the biotic community—animals, plants, and the whole of nature. Bioethical principles in food production and consumption are the keys to a more sensible, compassionate, and healthy future.

An increasingly monopolistic control over how our food is grown, processed, and marketed is a fact of the times that has implications in terms of consumer choice and right to know, and in terms of our health and the health of our animal companions. As consumers and public citizens (see Chapter 10), we must all take a stand, by voting with our dollars, and support those good farmers and food retailers who know that, as chef Alice Waters observes, good food starts in fields and orchards well tended. This is knowledge that we ignore at our peril, for without good farming there can be no good food; and without good food there can be no good life.

With bioethics, knowledge, and conscientious choices, we can all make a change for a better life, for the good life, for ourselves and our animal companions.

Chapter 4

Digestibility, Bioavailability, and All that Academic Stuff

Digestibility: Fresh Is Better

The digestive process is very complex when one considers how one mouthful of broccoli or steak, within a period of twelve to twenty-four hours after it enters your mouth, is broken down within the digestive tract into essential and nonessential amino acids, simple sugars, essential and nonessential fatty acids, glycerol, vitamins, and macro and micro minerals. These nutrients enter the bloodstream and are directed by hormones, the nervous system, and by various chemical reactions into the metabolic pathways that sustain your living body. No wonder the marketers for the pet food industry focus on the digestibility of their diets as a key promotional feature.

Digestibility is a measure of how much a particular nutrient is digested in the stomach and intestines and absorbed through the intestinal wall into the body. Bioavailability measures how much of a particular ingredient is actually utilized to support an animal's metabolism.

In the conventional pet food industry, the ingredients are byproducts of the agricultural industry and are subjected to heat during production of the base meal, and then again during the manufacturing and the extrusion process that results in the kibbles the animals eat. As the result of this dual processing, the overall digestibility of the various nutrients is only about 75 percent to 80 percent, and the bioavailability of the individual nutrients is less. Canned pet foods, which may contain up to 85 percent water, are considered more digestible (80 percent to 90 percent) but the high water content makes such foods more costly in terms of the actual density and amount of essential nutrients per pound, compared to more concentrated dried (and freeze-dried) foods. In other words, you may be paying a high price for a lot of water made into a gravy with artificial thickeners.

Less information is available for pet foods made up of primary fresh ingredients, the same foods we would eat at our table, because pet food manufacturing research has, for economic reasons, focused more on analyzing byproducts and synthetic additives than on fresh, whole-food ingredients. Individually these ingredients are highly digestible and the bioavailability is also high, both ranging from 85 percent to 100 percent. Minerals and vitamins contained in fresh food are more available to your pet than the ones used to supplement the commercial pet foods, because they are in a natural form and are more easily assimilated than synthetic, manufactured analogs. Thus to apply AAFCO standards to these pet foods is inappropriate and potentially misleading. This is because the AAFCO nutrient requirements are based on the minimum requirements necessary for a particular life stage and are drawn from the available literature based on studies in which commercially manufactured diets containing byproducts were fed and evaluated, as distinct from fresh whole food ingredients.

Role of the Gastrointestinal Tract

The evolution of the gastrointestinal (or alimentary/digestive) tract to accommodate the digestion of primarily plants and fiber to primarily protein and fat is fascinating. The two extreme states are seen in the herbivore and the carnivore with the omnivore combining some degree of both.

Digestion involves the breakdown of foodstuffs within the lumen (inside cavity) of the gastrointestinal tract into smaller packages that can pass into the intestinal epithelial cells that line the inside of the intestine for further processing and eventual utilization by the body.

This whole process requires specific environmental conditions provided by:

- Salivary glands, the pancreas, and the liver, which provide electrolytes, water, digestive enzymes, and bile salts.

   • Gut and gastric mucosa, which secrete an acid or a base
    to maintain optimal pH for digestive enzyme function.

The secretion of the above and the peristaltic contractions in the wall of the intestine that mixes the food and moves it down the tract is an energy-consuming process under the control of specific gastrointestinal hormones and the nerves from the spinal cord.

Epithelial digestion involves the absorption of the processed nutrients by the cells in the wall of the intestines, which transfer these nutrients into the blood. Also involved is the reabsorption of the water and electrolytes secreted to aid in the digestive process.

Gastrointestinal microorganisms are present in the colon. Organisms found within the stomach and small intestine are often ones that cause diseases when an abnormal luminal environment exists. A healthy colon has a diverse and complex bacterial population, the majority of which are anaerobes (meaning they do not require oxygen).

During the fermentation of undigested amino acids, compounds are produced (ammonia, aliphatic amines, insoles, phenols and volatile sulfur-containing compounds) that cause malodorous feces and gas. These compounds have been implicated in colonic cancer and the ammonia produced during this fermentation can cause health problems when kidney function is already impaired, as in many older animals. Prebiotics such as fructoligosaccharides and inulin have been used to increase the bifid bacteria and lactobacillus population and reduce ammonia production.

Enzymes are an important component of a normal digestive process. The activity and spectrum of enzymes present are dependent on the type and concentration of the substrates that they break down and the pH (degree of acidity/alkalinity) of their environment in the digestive tract. Enzymes can change as the substrates associated with age-related diet changes occur. Nursing puppies can digest the lactose in milk but as their diet changes they become lactose intolerant. And speaking of lactose intolerance, contrary to popular myth, adult cats cannot digest milk.

It's All about Calories! But Just Try to Count Them

Calories are a popular topic in the press and in our daily conversations. But if we were examined on what the term means and how calories are measured and applied we would likely fail. One thing we do know about calories is that if an animal eats too many it will get fat and if it eats too few it will lose weight. However, there is a lot more to be learned if we wish to sort the facts from fiction when it comes to the marketing of pet foods.

Many people, including veterinarians, find this aspect of nutrition the most difficult to understand. Adding to the confusion, many countries use different units to express energy requirements. Several different terms are used to describe the energy requirements of a pet and these can lead to some confusion when pet foods are evaluated. Energy intake is measured in calories, but what we call a calorie in regular conversation is technically a kilocalorie (Kcal), which equals 1,000 calories.

Go and get the container that you use to measure the amount of food for your pet and a small kitchen scale and a set of measuring cups. Then fill the container with the amount your pet is fed in a day and weigh the food. Now read the manufacturer's recommendations on the pet food package. Measure out that amount and weigh it. Are the two close? If not, then you may have an overweight or malnourished pet. Congratulations if your pet's weight is within normal range.

Energy is required to fuel the activities of the body. During this process, some energy is lost as heat from the body. Environmental temperature, metabolic activity (pregnancy, lactation), disease, functional demands, and age also influence energy needs. The energy or caloric requirement of an individual dog or cat is at best an educated guess and the calculated requirements often miss the true requirements by 50 percent. The nutrients in the diet must be balanced in relation to the caloric density of the diet. Some specialized diets are known as energy-dense diets.

How Much Should I Feed My Pet?

Each individual pet's daily caloric requirement is based on the pet's level of activity, age, and body condition. Determining the correct calorie requirements can be a challenging task, not

What Are Energy-Dense Diets?

These diets have the animal's nutritional and caloric requirements wrapped in a smaller package. The average maintenance dog food has an energy density of 350 to 375 kilocalories in 100 grams of food. Performance, premium, growth, and lactation diets usually have an energy density between 400 and 450 kilocalories per 100 grams. These foods contain more fat than the maintenance diets and are primarily fed to lactating dogs or those involved in hard work or endurance races. The average family pet would rapidly become obese if fed these diets. When energy-dense diets are fed, the directions concerning the daily amounts should be strictly followed. If these diets are overfed, a toxicity of some nutrients could occur over time. If underfed, a deficiency of these nutrients may develop.

only to the pet owner but to the veterinarian as well. An adequate nutrient intake and nutrients in the diet must be balanced to calorie content (energy density).

Whatever feeding strategy is chosen, the key to success is to meet the animal's energy or caloric requirements. If these caloric requirements are exceeded the pet will gain weight, if deficient, the pet will lose weight and remain hungry. The animal's appetite is a good indicator as to how much should be fed. Healthy and well-nourished animals will eat until they reach satiety. Any leftover food in the bowl means the serving was too large. If they eat ravenously and want more, the amount served should be slightly increased. Taking your pet's weight every week when on a new diet and having at least an annual veterinary check-up are important steps to determining if the animal is too fat or malnourished.

There are several methods for weighing your pet. A baby scale is ideal for cats or small dogs. If you have a regular bathroom scale, the best method is to weigh yourself, write down the number, then weigh yourself again while holding your pet, then subtract your weight from the total weight. A third method is to take your pet into your vet once a week. Most vets are glad to weigh your pet for free, with no appointment necessary.

Free feeding a dog or cat by allowing the animal to eat as much as it cares to within a specific time interval may be ideal. But ad libitum feeding, where food is available to the animal twenty-four hours a day from a dispenser, is not appropriate, especially for the couch-potato pet. Such a feeding regimen may be appropriate in rare instances, as for a working dog guarding a flock of sheep on a large pasture.

When Should I Feed My Pet?

A mature dog can be fed once a day if the amount meets its energy requirements. But many prefer twice-a-day feeding. No matter what the feeding pattern is, the owner should be consistent from day to day.

Cats prefer to eat numerous small meals per day, generally four to six small servings, and even up to twenty, if servings are very small and divided throughout the day. A twenty-four-hour allotment of food may be made available and the cat allowed to eat when it wishes from a dry-food dispenser. This is a popular convenience, but can mean obesity for many cats, and the risks of addiction to dry food and associated health problems are discussed in Chapters 6 and 7.

The owner's lifestyle and biases influence how his or her pet is fed. Some people with long work hours may substitute treats for the affection and exercise they just don't have time to give their pets. This can lead to obesity, as well as a listless and depressed pet. Dogs and cats alone all day often suffer from separation anxiety and boredom that can lead to overeating, especially when there is free access to an ad lib supply of dry food all day and nothing to do. The convenience of a quick and easy feeding regimen should not jeopardize the pet's health. And while you may feel you need that bowl of ice cream after a hard day at work, your pet definitely does not need one.

Ideally the owner and the pet will settle into a daily routine that will satisfy both. With a young, still growing kitten or puppy, a busy owner needs to find some way to provide food, affection, and play during the workday. For bonding, the ideal would be to get home during lunch break, or take the animal to work. But having a neighbor or professional care provider, or pet sitter, come by to feed and pay attention to young pets at least once a day during the work week is a worthwhile expense. Another alternative for dogs is doggy day care, a business available in many communities now, which is run much like child day care. Pups and adult dogs should be walked outdoors at least once during the working hours and should never be kept crated all day. This is an increasingly popular practice, and is an unwarranted cruelty.

Adjusting your lifestyle and expectations to better accommodate the animal's basic physical and emotional needs can not only provide you with much enjoyment of the pet's company, but can also do much to help prevent a number of health and behavioral problems. You may then also avoid having to put your pet on one of the expensive prescription diets that are widely accepted by many veterinarians—but you and your vet will have second thoughts about these once you have read the next chapter.

Chapter 5

Veterinary Prescription Foods

When a healthy dog or cat loses weight from a low caloric intake, the body adjusts by burning stored body fat as an energy source. A pet with chronic disease burns or metabolizes muscle as an energy source. This affects muscle strength, immune function, and survival. Although we understand what causes this, and in part through special diets we can slow down the process, we cannot yet reverse it.

It was a sad day for coauthor Meg Smart when her thirteen-year-old border collie was euthanized. The dog's loyalty, tenacity, and gentleness will forever be remembered. The collie was active until a month before her death, when Smart noticed that she was not going with the family to tend the sheep. The diagnosis was a mass in her lungs, and the prognosis was grave. Over the next few weeks, she wasted away and became progressively weaker. She was a victim of the malnutrition associated with chronic disease.

Vaccines, antibiotics, fungicides, pesticides, and herbicides can control harmful organisms (viruses, bacteria, fungi, and parasites). But these indiscriminate weapons can also destroy beneficial organisms, bodily functions and cells, and thus upset the natural balance.

Survival is a constant battle. A war is being waged that usually goes unnoticed, unless the enemy gains temporary or permanent control. Upon invasion of a harmful organism, host cells attracted to the site produce chemicals that alert the body's defense mechanisms. In a minor skirmish, these cells alone can wall off and control the infection.

If the infection is serious, a fever develops to make the environment too hot for the invading organism to reproduce. Nutrients, necessary for the organism's survival, relocate to storage sites until the skirmish is over. The host may stop eating for a short period so that a new supply of nutrients is not available. If the organism has invaded previously, antibodies are quickly produced to kill it. Antibody production against a previous invader occurs quickly. If a new organism invades, new antibody production and the establishment of a memory bank in the immune cells to control future invasions occur.

Sometimes the organism overcomes this defense and sets up camp within the host. If the host's defense mechanisms are compromised by malnutrition, stress or other diseases (diabetes, cancer, AIDS, etc.), it becomes easier for invaders to establish themselves. The established invader alters the host's metabolism for its own benefit. The host retains some of its defense strategies, often benefiting the invader.

Protein from the invalid's own muscles supplies amino acids for the growth of the invader, as well as energy for the host to nourish the troops and produce the chemicals to fight the war. Fat tissue cells provide fatty acids as an alternate energy supply, thus conserving glucose, the only energy source for the brain. Eventually, the host loses weight and the muscles waste away.

The tight binding of iron in storage cells to deprive the invader of this essential mineral may cause the host to develop chronic anemia. The host's appetite often becomes depressed, which complicates the picture. With all the hostility and breakdown of tissues occurring, valuable minerals are lost through urine and perspiration, and none are absorbed to replace them. Medical and nutritional intervention can shift the battle in favor of the host and eventually defeat the invader.

This simplistic overview outlines the complex nature of disease and the importance of a holistic approach. Progress in controlling life-threatening conditions will be limited if the nutritional and physiological components of disease are ignored. But are commercial veterinary medical foods, the so-called prescription diets, the solution?

The Origin of Veterinary Medical Foods

In 1939, a visionary veterinarian, Mark L. Morris, Sr., believed that certain diseases could be managed by appropriately formulated diets where the nutrients selected supported the body's ability to respond. He had an opportunity to test his theory when a blind man named Morris Frank brought his guide dog, Buddy, to him for treatment. Buddy had renal failure. Because of this encounter, the first veterinary prescription diet was formulated, and Hill's Pet Nutrition was founded.

Today, there are a handful of pet food companies whose scope is international:

- **Hill's Pet Food Company** (hillspet.com)

  The company was inspired by a guide dog. In 1939, Dr. Mark L. Morris, Sr. believed certain diseases in pets could be managed through carefully formulated diets. Now owned by Colgate-Palmolive Co.

- **Iams Company** (iamsco.com)

  In 1946, Paul Iams, an animal nutritionist, started the company in a small feed mill near Dayton, Ohio. His aim was to formulate a diet better than that available in grocery stores. Now owned by Proctor & Gamble, Inc.

- **Purina** (purina.com)

  Founded in 1893 by William H. Danforth, a pioneer in the commercial livestock feed industry, the idea was that animals must eat year round. In 1926, Purina developed diets for the hunting and working dogs of their rural clients. In 1950, Danforth started to apply the knowledge of farm animal nutrition to the development of a more nutritious and palatable dog food sold through grocery stores. In 1957, Purina Dog Chow entered national distribution. Now owned by Nestlés, Inc.

Mars Inc. (mars.com)

  Founded by Frank Mars in 1911, who with his wife Ethel, started to sell butter cream candies from their home in Tacoma, Washington. In 1930, Forrest

Mars pioneered the development of the European pet food industry, combining modern manufacturing techniques with nutritional science. Now owned by MasterFoods.

Unfortunately, the way these corporations have set up their pet food branches, the consumer still thinks of them as small family-run businesses and not as part of large multinational conglomerates.

Veterinary Medical Foods

The term "medical food" was defined under the 1983 United States Orphan Drug Act as food that is formulated to be consumed or administered under the supervision of a physician and intended for the specific dietary management of a disease or condition for which distinctive nutritional requirements, based on sound scientific principles, are established by medical evaluation."

Although originally intended as a guide for human foods, medical foods formulated as a sole source of nutrition for pets with a specific medical condition come under the same umbrella.

These veterinary medical foods are subject to the same labeling requirements as any pet food. Veterinary medical foods must have on the label a statement of nutritional adequacy formulated to meet AAFCO nutrient profiles or passed an AAFCO-designed feeding trial for a particular life stage. Diets that do not qualify for this label must be labeled for intermittent or supplemental feeding only. Veterinary medical foods are exempt from the requirement to include feeding directions on the label as they are used under veterinary supervision.

Ideally, veterinary medical foods with treatment claims should be classified as drugs and subject to the normal premarket clearance protocol to show safety and efficacy. A caveat exists when it comes to veterinary medical foods; the FDA has decided to use "regulatory discretion" in order for the consumer to get some meaningful health-related information.

Mountains of information can be found on the Internet about "pet foods" in general, but the information about "veterinary medical diets" is minuscule in comparison (1,310,000 Google hits vs. 694 hits).

Currently the four major multinational companies mentioned above sell these veterinary medical foods worldwide.

Some smaller U.S. companies such as Wysong Rx and Affinity Pet Care-Advanced Veterinary Diets that at present sell their diets only within the United States have plans to expand into other countries.

Over the past year, the four major manufacturers of veterinary prescription diets have updated their websites. These websites were updated in part due to the Menu Foods recall detailed in Chapter 2. In some cases, the updates reflect changes in the formulation of the diet or in the company's structure related to mergers and acquisitions. These companies maintain websites for veterinarians about the details of the diet and the research in support of their diets, in the form of fact sheets, technical bulletins, and scientific articles. For the layperson, each company provides a brief description of the product, the features of the diet, and the medical problems that can benefit from these diets, but stresses that these diets are available through veterinarians only.

Research Funding

A recent article in *Discover* magazine, "Science under Siege," focused on pharmaceutical research, but it also sheds light on what happened to the pet food industry in 1976, when Colgate-Palmolive purchased Hill's. Big pharmaceutical companies provided private funding to academic institutions, thus enabling them to employ science and scientists in their fight against regulation. Research in small animal nutrition has been traditionally underfunded or, more accurately, seldom funded by independent granting agencies. This has left the field wide open for the pet food industry to control and direct the research done in academic institutions and within their own facilities, meaning that research into pet foods is seldom at arm's length in terms of scientific objectivity and impartiality.

Understanding and Interpreting Pet Food Research and Development

Research into the nutritional requirements of companion animals is not as straightforward as it is in livestock nutrition. In food-animal trials, a relatively uniform group of animals is used, and the end point of the experiments is set with defined production parameters that are measured, statistically compared, and conclusions drawn. Although all animal trials must have prior approval by affiliated Animal Care Committees to ensure humane treatment, livestock trials often end with the humane slaughter of the animals and their tissues are harvested for detailed analysis.

For veterinary medical foods, in the past, and to a limited degree now, experimental animals were surgically altered (for example, having kidneys partially removed) or were fed poisons to damage a specific organ, like the liver or kidneys, in order to evaluate the response of that animal to nutritional intervention. Although the results are still used to justify the formulation of some veterinary medical foods, do they actually represent the progression of a natural disease? Companion animal experiments in the past may have ended with the euthanasia and necropsy of the animal, but today this type of conclusion to a pet food test is not acceptable in the public's eye.

The validity of trials conducted on dogs and cats kept in a kennel or research facility is also questionable, since such animals do not have the same freedoms and human bonding experiences of the pets kept within a home environment. Most nutritional trials on companion animals are only valid for that particular group, maintained under the same conditions and fed identical diets. Even the results from the relatively simple noninvasive digestibility, palatability and feeding trials done in kennels or catteries, specifically established and approved to conduct these trials, have come under scrutiny when environment, previous diet, gender, breed and age differences are considered (see Appendix C).

Bringing This All Together

Initially this chapter was to be a comparative analysis of veterinary prescription diets. Such a study seemed like a simple task: Take the product keys and the Internet information on the company and their products in particular, check the research behind their claims and indications, and then interpret the findings in relationship to Figure 1 (see Appendix C). This gives you a tool with which to draw meaningful conclusions from the companies' products and recommendations.

After three years of study, countless spreadsheets, direct communications with the companies' contacts, and revisions associated with the recent changes in the product keys, massive amounts of data and comparison tables have been generated by coauthor Smart, with few concrete conclusions drawn. If an academic professor and veterinarian finds this study almost impossible to complete, how can busy small animal clinicians in private practice give informed and unbiased advice on the diets sold within their practices? By default, they have become reliant on the manufacturers of the diets they sell to their clients to provide this information.

General Information about Veterinary Medical Foods/Prescription Diets

Confusion results from the manufacturers using such terms in their product keys as: added, reduced, low, excessive, high, adequate. They do not indicate what these mean in relationship to a specific value of published minimum or maximum requirements.

The 2006 National Research Council (NRC) requirements for cats and dogs complicate the picture by expressing nutrient requirements as minimal, adequate intake, recommended allowance, and safe upper limit. The Association of American Feed Control Officials nutrient profiles primarily list minimum or maximum requirement percentages. These descriptors could have significant meaning, if the industry adopted the NRC and/or AAFCO as the gold standard. For example: For renal diets, if the descriptors for low or reduced protein were revised to meet NRC's minimal requirements for protein or AAFCO's minimum protein percentages, this would have more meaning to the veterinarian who could then advise the client if the dog finds the prescription diet not palatable or if the client is looking for an alternative homemade diet.

A statement of nutritional adequacy is a label requirement. But this statement is seldom found in the product keys or the promotional material, including the websites, so the dog owner could end up feeding a diet labeled for supplemental or intermittent use long term, if he or she doesn't read the actual package label. But if this information is included on all the available materials, both the veterinarian and client can understand the long-term impact the diet may have. This is particularly true if the diet had been subjected to feeding trials. A nutritional adequacy statement would put veterinary medical foods on a par with commercial diets.

Most of the product keys claim that the diets contain highly digestible ingredients, yet after the examination of the entire veterinary medical foods ingredient lists, most of the first five ingredients are common to the manufacturer's OTC (over the counter) or regular diets. So the digestibility of ingredients is not likely to be any different from the OTC diets. Do not confuse a small or large stool (bowel movement) with digestibility, as it is more a reflection of the fiber content of the diet than of the digestibility of nutrients in the diet.

Closely linked to digestibility is palatability. Pet owners assume a very palatable diet is good for the pet because he or she likes it. But veterinary medical foods are historically not very palatable. To improve the palatability, flavors are added, usually with fat. In many veterinary medical foods, even the weight loss diets, if the manufacturer's feeding recommendations are followed daily, fat intake often exceeds the daily requirements. A 20-pound adult dog requires approximately 8 grams of fat per day in a maintenance diet, and the added fat in these special diets can do more harm than good.

Examples:

- Renal diets provide an average of 26 grams of fat per day in the dry food formulations and 29 grams in the canned, or about three times the recommended amount. These diets are already restricted in protein, so if the pet is overweight or has chronic pancreatitis, a renal diet may not be appropriate, and is potentially harmful.
- Weight loss diets provide a 20-pound mature couch potato dog on average 8.6 grams of fat per day, the canned 13.3 grams, still well over the recommended amount. This amount is equivalent to AAFCO's minimum intake for dry diets and exceeds the daily requirements for the canned diets. Although the diets may comply

with AAFCO's definition of weight control diets, terms of reduced or low fat used in the promotio materials and product keys have very little meaning.

Obesity Diets

The necessity for special diets for weight reduction and control in pets is a myth perpetuated by the pet food manufacturers capitalizing on our human obsessions with food and dieting. The myth that all these diets are necessary for the pet to receive a complete and balanced diet while achieving a healthy weight is not logical. The truth is as simple as it is with humans: too many calories eaten, not enough calories expended. Only the wealthy nations of the world spend money to put weight on and then to take it off, both the people and their pets.

Although consumers spend countless dollars in the pursuit of the perfect diet, these are seldom successful without behavior modification and a will to succeed. The biggest difference between our pets and ourselves is that we have control of what and when we eat; our pets do not. Who benefits from this situation? Perhaps we need to question the motives of an industry that profits when the weight is put on and again when it is taken off, a definite boost for the shareholders. All the major players manufacture veterinary and OTC adult diets for maintenance, weight control, and weight loss.

Yet where does the pet owner receive information on how much and what to feed their dogs and cats? From the sales clerk at the store, from the manufacturer's recommendations on the label, from pet health professionals, or from researching the literature in pet nutrition? From guessing?

AAFCO has developed recommendations for weight loss product labels, where "light" is defined as dry diets containing less than 310 Kcal/100g and 900 Kcal/100g on a dry matter basis for canned. But how much does your particular pet need? And do you have the time and talent to do the math?

Purina Life Long Study

In 2002, at the Purina Pet Institute symposium, "Advancing Life Through Diet Restriction," the results of their twelve-yearudy on Labrador retrievers were presented. A more accurate title for this would have been "Advancing Life Through Calorie Control." This massive study involved the measurement of metabolic processes involved with growth and aging. In the trial, the restricted fed (RF) dogs received 75 percent of the same diet consumed by the control fed (CF) group, which was fed ad libitum (all they could eat in 15 minutes).

Conclusions and recommendations from this study:

- Median life span of RF dogs was 13 years, and 11.2 years in the CF dogs, but mortality causes were the same in both groups.
- Diet restriction retarded several age-related immune changes.
- At 2 years of age, the RF dog had less hip dysplasia (subluxation) in the hip joint, and in these lean dogs the onset of osteoarthritis was delayed, and the severity and incidence was lower.
- A body fat of less than 22 percent is a reasonable goal to attain maximum quality of life and longevity.

The bottom line was that owners should adjust the caloric intake of a puppy or mature dog to maintain an ideal body condition based on Nestlé Purina Body Condition System where the ideal condition is: Waist when viewed from above is easily seen, ribs are easily felt, the skin is loose over the ribs indicating some fat over ribs.

Recommended Nutrient Intakes for Managing Obesity

- Increasing dietary protein in exchange for carbohydrates can be beneficial.
- Low calorie diets with an increased protein-to-calorie ratio increase the percentage of fat lost and maintain lean body mass.
- Fiber can be used to dilute or reduce caloric density of the diet, providing a measure of satiety or fullness.
- Water can dilute calories per volume of food. Canned foods contain between 70 and 82 percent water, and

on a dry matter basis they may have higher fat and calorie content, but they have a lower caloric density on an as-fed basis.

- L-carnitine supplementation is likely beneficial if the diet lacks the methionine and lysine precursors. Carnitine facilitates the oxidation of fatty acids. Under normal conditions carnitine supplementation is of limited value. In diets supplemented with L-carnitine at 50 and 100mg/kg of diet, weight loss was increased. Check with your veterinarian about this.

Owner Education

A study on the value of owner education on nutrition-related topics found that over a six-month weight loss period, followed by an eighteen-month weight maintenance period, and a monthly weight check, a mean weight loss of 15 percent was achieved.

Nutrition and the Kidney

The kidney acts as the body's "clearinghouse," conserving vital minerals, degrading and excreting harmful metabolic byproducts, controlling water balance, acid-base balance, blood pressure, and producing hormones such as vitamin D (bone metabolism), erythropoietin (red blood cell production), and rennin. Thus, when the kidney fails, a number of organs and metabolic pathways are affected.

Coauthor Smart's introduction to chronic kidney disease was a traumatic learning experience. It occurred while she was a student working in a small animal practice in Chicago. One morning a client brought his cocker spaniel in for a bath and clip. He brought the dog in a closed box because the dog smelled bad. After the client left, the box was opened and the smell was overwhelming. The dog growled and showed his teeth in a very unfriendly way, so a gauze muzzle was made. The dog snapped at the gauze and when the gauze was pulled out, most of his teeth also came out tangled in the gauze. The dog immediately died. How would the owner take this? Was this the end of a promising veterinary career? It turns out the foul smell was ammonia and the loose teeth were related to the loss of bone mineral (rubber jaw), all caused by severe, chronic, and untreated kidney failure.

A vocation was saved.

Controversy continues over the ideal diet for dogs with renal (kidney) failure. Most of the nutritional trials reported in the literature used healthy young dogs with surgically compromised renal function, which in reality does not always mimic the true progression of kidney disease. Renal diets are formulated to improve the pet's quality of life by alleviating or slowing down development of the clinical signs associated with a uremic crisis when toxic levels of ammonia are in the bloodstream. In general, early kidney diets restricted protein, phosphorus and sodium intakes. Although most diets still restrict protein, the necessity for this is debatable. Such restricted diets not only can lead to nutritional deficiencies over the long term but also cannot be fed to puppies.

The response to such diets depends on the cause, location of disease in the kidney, and duration and severity of the kidney damage. New formulations of renal diets to control the rise in serum phosphorous, restrict phosphorous absorption, and supplement with omega-3 fatty acids to improve flow through the kidney blood-filters, the so-called glomeruli.

The Gold Standard

A prospective clinical trial by Dr. D. Polzin compared a renal failure diet to an adult maintenance diet. This trial is used now by the manufacturers of kidney diets to justify the nutrient levels of the current renal diets. This trial is also cited as the highest quality evidence when using the evidence-based approach to patient therapy. This study concluded that the delay in the development of uremic crises and associated mortality rate in dogs fed a renal failure diet was associated in part with the reduction in rate of progression of renal failure. The diets were fed at home by the owners with no disruption in the daily feeding schedule, with checkups and renal evaluation panels done at regular intervals. The trial lasted for two years.

The Other Side of the Story:
Is this Research the Best Quality Evidence?

This trial has several limitations related to diet selection and feeding regime. The maintenance diet chosen for this trial is equivalent to a premium all life stage diet, thus the response in the dog will depend on its total daily caloric intake and whether one meal per day or several small meals were fed during the day. If a veterinarian were choosing a maintenance diet for a dog with signs of early renal failure, or a dog that is genetically at risk to develop progressive renal disease, this "adult maintenance" diet would not be inappropriate, but a more appropriate diet would be a true maintenance diet with a dietary protein of 5g/100Kcal and phosphorous of 140mg/100Kcal. Each diet should have been provided in small amounts three or more times per day if possible.

Fructoligosaccharides (FOS) have been advocated to trap nitrogen in the colon by increasing the microbial population, which utilizes nitrogen for their own protein metabolism. This nitrogen is not absorbed and thus does not contribute to an increased blood urea nitrogen, a serious problem in animals with diseased kidneys.

The sources of ingredients in the renal diets differ very little from the OTC commercial diets, despite the manufacturers' claim that the protein sources are of high quality. Of the animal-based protein sources, egg and egg byproducts (although often listed as a highly digestible protein source in the product key), do not appear before the fifth listed ingredient in most of the renal diets, with the exception of Hill's Diets. The ingredient list would not be helpful in evaluating these diets.

Unfortunately, no standard has been set to help the pet owner or veterinarian quantify and interpret what is meant by the terms "reduced" and "low." In terms of the daily intake of protein, most values fall between the NRC's recommended allowance and AAFCO's minimum recommendations. All diets fall below AAFCO minimum recommended allowance for phosphorous and most fall below the NRC's recommended allowances. The fat intake in most diets is greater than three times the NRC's recommended allowance. If the dog is already overweight, these diets will only perpetuate the problem. Because of the low dietary phosphorus intake, these diets are labeled for intermittent and supplemental feeding only.

The Bottom Line

If your dog is diagnosed with early signs of renal disease based on blood results taken during a wellness examination, there is no reason to immediately start to feed a renal diet, as an OTC adult maintenance diet is adequate. The amount fed during the day could be divided and be fed twice or more times per day. Renal diets appear to be beneficial when the serum phosphorous starts to increase. At no time should these diets be fed to puppies.

Growth Diets

The research cited to support the dietary recommendations for large breed puppies appears to be misrepresented when it comes to the formulation and marketing of growth diets. The growth rate in puppies and the eventual mature body weight are genetically controlled. In large breed puppies, how rapidly the puppy reaches 80 percent of its adult body weight is controlled by its diet. Fat puppies are cute puppies but not necessarily healthy puppies. Many owners like to brag about how rapidly their puppy is growing. But it is likely that these dogs, by the time they are 4 years old, will have had at least one bout of lameness, radiographs positive for hip dysplasia, or require surgery for hip joint disintegration (osteochondrosis dissecans), or cruciate knee-ligament repair.

A comparison of more than fifty dry puppy diets, including veterinary prescription diets, revealed that some large breed puppy diets might be marginal or deficient in calcium relative to the caloric density. If these diets are fed according to manufacturers' recommendations, the calcium intake of these puppies may be marginal or deficient. These same diets, if fed to meet a puppy's caloric requirements, will exceed NRC's and AAFCO's dietary requirements for fat, which could lead to the puppy becoming fat. If these diets are restricted to control weight, the calcium intake will be even less.

Most veterinary nutritionists and manufacturers contend that the overriding factor to all feeding recommendations is the body condition of the puppy. Various charts and descriptions are available to assist the veterinarian and the client in evaluating the puppy's body condition. In most cases, the amount fed is based on the owner's judgment and perception of what a puppy shou look like. How the owner defines a 1-cup measurement is anothe factor governing the puppy's daily caloric intake. Findings that some puppy diets are marginal in calcium and phosphorous, if they are fed according to the manufacturer's recommendations, indicates that the decision to further restrict the caloric intake could contribute to the future development of orthopedic disease.

Food Allergy Diets

Diet-related allergies in pets seem to be increasing. Many theories have been proposed but few answers have been found. True food allergies are defined as an immune-mediated adverse reaction to primarily protein antigens ingested in food. Food intolerances are also considered an adverse reaction to foods. These are not immune mediated and may be induced by toxins, drugs, or chemicals.

As people and their pets become urbanized, exposure within the environment to beneficial microorganisms present on the skin and populating the gastrointestinal tract and the upper respiratory system may decrease. These bacteria, along with the immune system, protect by shielding us from the invasion of harmful microorganisms, and may even block irritating chemicals, or neutralize abnormal chemical reactions. This lack of exposure and inadequate colonization of various parts of the body by beneficial microorganisms may leave the skin and respiratory and digestive systems vulnerable to these noxious agents.

The allergic reactions to commercial kibble diets may in part be related to an immune-mediated response to the protein-starch gelatinized molecules within the kibble. Often switching the pet to a minimally processed whole food diet may resolve the problem. This can be accomplished without going through costly allergy and diet elimination tests.

The commercial hypoallergenic diets are formulated to provide a single unique protein source or a hydrolyzed protein molecule broken down to be small enough to not cause an allergic response.

It is notable that in June 2008, the executive board of the American Veterinary Medical Association approved policy changes ᴀrged by the Council on Biologic and Therapeutic Agents in the ᴌabeling claims on the above kinds of manufactured prescription foods for dogs and cats. It was agreed that the FDA should require pet foods with health claims to include a statement indicating that the FDA has not evaluated such claims.

While this chapter has focused primarily on the serious limitations of veterinary medical foods/prescription diets for sick pets, with particular reference to dogs, the basic, and unique, nutritional needs of cats in sickness and in health will be covered in the next four chapters.

Chapter 6

The Predator Among Us:
How Cats Are Unique

On April 12, 2007, coauthor Elizabeth Hodgkins was privileged to find herself in a unique and challenging situation. She had been asked by the office of United States Senator Richard Durbin to testify in a Senate hearing called by the Agriculture Appropriations subcommittee. This meeting began the governmental inquiry into the massive pet food recall that had commenced a month earlier when Menu Foods, a Canadian company and major co-packer of commercial cat and dog foods for many of the world's pet food companies, announced the largest single pet food recall in history.

As a veterinarian of thirty years, she had worked for nearly a decade at one of the largest U.S. pet food companies, and had assigned a patent for a novel cat food to another very large pet food company. In her testimony before the subcommittee, she told the senators that she believed commercial pet foods were inadequately regulated by the federal government, and that pet foods carried unsubstantiated health and safety claims. Hodgkins urged the senators to strengthen regulation of this industry and to review all health and safety claims on pet foods as they would review such claims made for human foods.

The Pet Food Industry in the United States

Unfortunately, pet foods are all but unregulated in the U.S. This is true today, and was certainly true in decades past when the manufacturers of livestock feeds first began to recognize that there was a growing market for commercial foods for pets. As this new market grew, the abundance of agricultural byproducts in this country presented the livestock feed companies with readily available and inexpensive ingredients for use in their new dog and cat foods.

Commercially processed dog foods preceded commercial cat foods, because the market for convenient bagged and canned canine diets was originally much larger than for cat foods. The omnivorous dog seemed to do relatively well, at least short-term, on the foods that pet food manufacturers produced from agricultural byproducts. Subsequently, the success of commercial dog foods spurred the new pet food manufacturers to expand their product lines to include foods for cats. The convenience of commercial products made these foods very popular with pet owners, who assumed that the manufacturers were producing foods that were wholesome for their pet dogs and cats.

The truth is, very little thought was given to what ought to be going onto commercial pet foods. At that time, there was literally no regulatory authority over the production of pet foods; if pets would eat a particular product, that was all that mattered to the manufacturers in this new industry. Over time, the Food and Drug Administration (FDA) assumed a nominal responsibility for overseeing the quality of pet foods. The FDA then delegated this responsibility to the American Association of Feed Control Officials (AAFCO), a loose group of state feed regulators who looked to the pet food industry for guidance about how to regulate this new class of product, commercial pet foods. Unfortunately, this was a matter of the fox guarding the henhouse.

Today, there are thousands of choices of these products to confuse and complicate the pet owner's selection. Making matters worse, there is almost no meaningful information on the labels of these products to help in that selection. This is because AAFCO, acting in accord with the pet food industry, has constructed a regulatory scheme in which meaningless tests are used to justify the nutritional safety and adequacy claims contained on every bag and can you find in the grocery store and pet food warehouse aisles. When pet food purchasers see the AAFCO complete and balanced statement on a label, they are misled to believe that the food in the package is carefully tested and found worthy of that governmental guarantee. Nothing could be further from the truth. *The lifetime safety and adequacy claims that what consumers read on the labels of most pet foods they buy have no valid scientific foundation.*

Furthermore, the legal definitions of pet food ingredients, which are completely and tightly controlled by AAFCO and the industry itself, are completely unintelligible to the pet food purchaser. For example (and this is only one of hundreds of such examples), meat byproducts can describe any of hundreds of different types of animal-source ingredients, varying from rendered condemned or diseased animal parts all the way to high-quality organ tissues from USDA-inspected processing plants. The pet food purchaser has no way to know the difference, and AAFCO forbids the use of any additional descriptive information on the label. Why would the pet food industry itself want such rigid control of what can be said on pet food labels? Wouldn't the individual companies want to have great freedom to tell prospective customers how wonderful their own products really are?

The truth is, the pet food industry is controlled by the largest companies, which are owned by multinational megacorporations. These companies have the resources to compete against each other on the basis of marketing dollars spent; they have no need to compete on the basis of product quality. The effectiveness of marketing, not the quality of products, creates consumer beliefs; we all know this fact of a free market economy. Therefore, it is far more cost effective for these very large companies to invest in advertising than to spend their money for better quality ingredients or product testing. With the large companies having no incentive to improve quality of pet foods, and strict regulatory constraints on smaller companies marketing their foods on the basis of better quality, the industry is essentially homogenized, and consumers are led to base all of their buying decisions on the most attractive labeling and most memorable television ads they see. Of course, the largest companies have the most attractive packaging and the biggest TV ad budgets.

If pet foods today were merely overpriced and excessively hyped in the marketplace, that would be bad enough. But the plain reality is that the formulation and manufacture of commercial pet foods today present a clear danger to the health of our pets, especially cats. More than any other species, our pet cats are most threatened because of their unique metabolic characteristics.

How did we get to this sad state of affairs? To understand the answer to this question, we must first consider just what makes cats so special and so vulnerable to life-threatening nutritional diseases caused by inadequate nutrition.

From their role as workers in charge of controlling the vermin population in a ranch, farm, or neighborhood setting, cats have recently become genuinely unemployed house pets, captive in the completely controlled environment of the home.

All of the major lethal diseases of our feline companions, including obesity, diabetes, bladder problems (including inflammatory cystitis), kidney failure, hyperthyroidism, inflammatory bowel disease, and even some forms of cancer are directly related to mistakes loving humans make in caring for their cats.

In the past, we humans provided certain protection to the local cats in exchange for the service of ridding our homes and towns of disease-carrying and grain-consuming rodents. In this historical relationship, it was not necessary, and not even particularly desirable, that the cat become a true pet. In this prior role, a cat's work required that it retain all of its keen, wild hunting instincts and hunger. The cat was left outdoors, seldom fed from the family's table, and was generally encouraged to remain feral in all aspects. For the cat to be of service to humans, it was logically necessary that it remain just as it was before the relationship with humankind began.

It is true that in a few ancient societies, the cat was revered, even deified, as in the Egypt of approximately 2000 BC, but there certainly is no historical evidence that deification altered in any way the cat's basic nature and metabolism during this period.

Some evidence from the ancient Middle East shows cats seeming to live in the homes of the Egyptians and even to assist in the hunting and killing of small game and fish. Tombs of cats from the Egypt of 4,000 years ago, however, show funerary offerings like milk, dead rodents, and other animal-source nutrition provided to accompany the mummified felines into the afterlife. The feline entombments of the time lack the much wider assortment of food types provided to mummified humans, suggesting that the Egyptians understood the natural inclinations of the cat in their relationship with this species.

The cat's unique, primitive metabolic and nutritional needs have not been changed through this simple process of adaptation to living closer to humans. The workings of the cat's mind and body remain intensely prehistoric, molded through thousands of years of selective environmental pressures into the perfect carnivore, the top predator of its environment. Nothing that humanity has done to harness the useful qualities of this predatory mammal has changed that in any way.

A true and strict (or obligatory) carnivore from the outset, the cat has not become more omnivorous as it began to live closer to humans, despite claims by some pet food companies to the contrary. This is an extremely important point. For the cat to have experienced a transition toward the omnivore lifestyle (like dogs), it would have needed some selective pressure for this change, such as a scarcity of a natural prey diet in the face of abundant vegetation, as well as the reproductive ability to pass on any mutations that might make certain individuals better adapted to a change from a meat diet to a vegetable-based diet. In decades past when cats lived outdoors, there was certainly no lack of small mammals and birds for those outdoor cats to hunt and eat, so there would have been no selective pressure for the species to become herbivorous, or at least more of an omnivore like us.

True enough, today's indoor cats are exposed, even forced, to consume diets with very high amounts of processed vegetable matter because they have no opportunity to hunt for themselves. Essentially, they live within an environment that puts selective pressure on them to adapt to this drastic change in diet. But today, we have almost entirely removed any opportunity for mutations that might make some cats more tolerant of this high carbohydrate diet to be passed to succeeding generations. Indoor cats that are forced to consume and survive off vegetable-based diets are almost always spayed or neutered. Even if there were individuals within the population of our pet cats who were genetically better suited to high carbohydrate diets, those cats do not pass on that capability to new generations of cats. The argument that house cats are somehow different from cats of times past in their ability to cope with an unnatural diet falls flat when we examine it scientifically.

The Difference Between Dogs and Cats

Dogs and cats have remarkably different, and highly specialized, anatomy. Dogs have forty-two permanent teeth while cats have only thirty. Dogs have more molars than cats, with specialized shape for crushing, associated with intake of plant material. In contrast, the shape of feline teeth is specialized for grasping and tearing flesh. By its structure, the cat's jaw has far more restricted mobility side-to-side and front-to-back than the dog's, limiting its ability to grind a varied vegetation-containing diet, as the dog can do. The cat's eyes and ears are positioned forward on the head to provide exquisite acuity of vision and hearing when tracking prey, particularly at night. Retractable claws, seen on cats but not dogs, are another specialized feature of an animal that must chase, catch and bring down all of its food in the form of wild prey.

The digestive tracts of the two species are also quite different. Those differences emphasize the differences in the natural diets of each. Science tells us that modifications in the basic structure of this important organ system from species to species are closely connected to the diet of each. The cat's stomach, caecum (appendix) and colon, segments of the digestive tract most associated with digestion of vegetable matter, are smaller than those of the dog. The length of the intestine in the cat in proportion to its body length is short compared to the dog, indicating that the cat's evolutionary diet was highly digestible (protein and fat) compared to that of the dog consuming far more vegetable matter. The inner lining of the cat's stomach has significantly greater surface area than the same part of the dog's stomach. Anatomists believe that increases in the relative size of this stomach area are an adaptation to the digestion of higher meat, more calorie-dense diets. The caecum in the cat is very primitive, while it is much better developed in the dog. Once again, this portion of the gastrointestinal tract assists in the processing of fibrous, non-meat dietary constituents.

We see strong evidence of the cat's strictly carnivorous origins in its nutrient requirements, especially its requirements for protein. In the 1970s and 1980s, scientists showed conclusively that kittens and cats need far more protein than puppies or adult dogs. Unlike the dog, the cat burns protein to make energy for its everyday use, all of the time. Most other animals, including humans, burn large amounts of protein for energy only when protein is plentiful in the diet.

In contrast, the cat has an ongoing high requirement for protein to turn into energy, even when dietary protein intake is very limited. During starvation or protein-restriction, the cat is forced to disassemble its body's own constituent proteins (enzymes, antibodies, organ tissues, etc.) to produce fuel for energy to keep the cells alive and functioning. Thus, in the most fundamental way, the health and tissue integrity of the cat is dependent upon the continual intake of highly digestible protein, especially protein from meat.

The cat also requires arachidonic acid, an essential fatty acid found only in meat, but not plants. And cats must consume preformed vitamin A from animal-source foods because they are unable to make this essential vitamin from the beta carotene found in plants. Dogs and humans can do this. There are many more such special dietary requirements that reflect feline evolutionary adaptations to a life as an obligatory carnivore.

The Cat's Liver Is Very Different

Perhaps the most fascinating special characteristic of the cat is the manner in which its liver functions. In fact, the cat's high protein and amino acid requirements arise from the constantly high activity of certain enzymes in the feline liver. These enzymes disassemble the amino acids in protein to make them available for the production of energy. The more omnivorous dog has a liver that is also capable of this function, but omnivores can turn the rate of this function up or down depending on how much dietary protein is available. In contrast, the cat has its liver protein burn rate turned to high at all times, even when dietary protein is scarce or entirely absent. Death from protein starvation can be very rapid in this species as a result.

In the liver, protein amino acids are processed into glucose (sugar) and sent into the bloodstream to supply the body's need for this energy nutrient. In a meat-eating species like the cat, the liver will manufacture the great majority of the animal's needed glucose, which is the primary energy supply for the brain. There is little glucose in a high-meat diet, so this is an essential task for an obligatory carnivore. On the other hand, the cat's liver has very limited ability to process dietary carbohydrate because there was little dietary carbohydrate in the cat's evolutionary environment. The livers of omnivores, including people and dogs, have multiple enzyme systems for handling dietary carbohydrate; the cat has only one such enzyme system with limited capacity to deal with high carbohydrate consumption.

As a result of all these specializations, the cat fits its ecological niche as a small predator perfectly. The most successful animal in a niche will be the one with the fewest and simplest systems for survival. The cat's ancestors did not need the ability to turn their livers' protein burn rates up and down or to handle high dietary carbohydrate so it dispensed with, or never evolved, most of these abilities.

The African Connection

The present-day house cat (Felis domesticus) is believed to have descended thousands of years ago from a small wild cat (Felis lybica) native to the deserts and savannahs of North Africa. Such a dry climate heritage would explain many of the other distinct characteristics of this species. Cats can survive for long periods without water, and will naturally consume very little free water when they are fed high water content canned cat food or fresh meat. They can produce urine that is highly concentrated compared to that of the dog and other animals that evolved in more water-rich environments. The cat's natural tendency to produce urine with a great deal of metabolic waste in a highly concentrated form can be dangerous if a cat feeds on a diet that is low in water (such as dry cat foods), because this desert animal has a naturally low thirst drive. A low thirst drive means that the cat has a poor thirst mechanism to tell it to drink more water when it is becoming dehydrated. This can be more of a problem for some cats than for others who like to drink plenty, especially from a dripping faucet! This low thirst drive can result in especially concentrated urine, which can then lead to medical problems, including certain kinds of bladder disease.

Why We Have Failed Our Cats

If we understand the cat's natural anatomy and physiology we can understand its needs for health and happiness. For all of their advanced intelligence, house cats cannot adjust to highly unnatural living circumstances any better than their much larger wild cousins on the African savannahs or the rain forests of Asia could. The so-called domestic cat is not fully domesticated. It is a small, essentially feral species, that has made only modest accommodations to living intimately with humans. No longer able to follow its natural instincts for obtaining food according to natural instincts, it has no choice but to try to get along on whatever we humans decide to provide.

Because we have made our cats entirely dependent upon us for their very lives, we bear an enormous responsibility to provide them what they really need, and not just what is convenient for us. Exotic zoo species like the "big cats, also captives and dependent upon humans for healthy survival, receive very carefully designed diets that conform to their individual, natural dietary needs. This is just common sense, if we wish to keep these animals healthy for their natural life spans. Similarly, there is no intelligent argument that captive pet cats should be expected to thrive on diets that are less carefully tailored to their specific requirements than the diets of captive lions and tigers. Even so, that is exactly how they are cared for today, with little regard for the nutrients and balance of nutrients that are so necessary for these housebound animals.

How has this happened? How have we managed to wander so far from the proper path of responsible stewardship of our pet cats? The answer lies in the nature of the pet food industry, and the drive for business profitability in a free market economy in which there are few if any constraints on that profitability.

In the chapters ahead, we will discuss how the lack of product quality in many commercial cat foods causes many of the most serious diseases veterinarians see in today's pet cats. We will also discuss how this information can help pet owners make better, more healthful decisions about how to nourish their family felines.

Pet Food Irradiation

In April 2001, State Departments of Agriculture announced that "The FDA approved an irradiation process that can be used on all animal feed and feed ingredients, including pet food and treats. This process can reduce the risk of contamination from all strains of Salmonella bacteria. Salmonella organisms can cause gastrointestinal upset and diarrhea in people and pets."

The government states: "Irradiation is a process in which products are exposed to sources of ionizing radiation which cause chemical, not nuclear, changes similar to other conventional cooking or preservation methods. It has already been approved for use on a variety of human foods. Extending this process to animal feed and feed ingredients will not only increase the safety of the feed for the animals consuming it, but to people who handle animal feed and feed ingredients. Irradiation is a useful tool for reducing disease risk."

But studies have shown that irradiation does affect the nutrient content of certain foods, destroying or denaturing enzymes, proteins, and certain vitamins, and produces so called radiolytic break-down products, the safety of which has not been determined. According to the Organic Consumer Association, "The FDA based its approval of irradiation to treat meat products on only 5 animal studies of 441 studies submitted, and these 5 either showed health effects or had obvious scientific flaws. In fact, animal studies have shown many health effects, such as tumors, kidney failure, death of offspring and miscarriages." Laboratory animal tests of the effects of irradiated food have reported embryonic deaths and lower offspring survival: internal bleeding (associated with Vitamin K deficiency); nutritional muscular dystrophy (associated with Vitamin E deficiency). Irradiated foods contain novel free radicals and other compounds with the potential to cause mutations and cancer, and the process can damage essential nutrients such as Vitamins A, C, B1, B2, B3, B6 and folic acid (www.organicconsumer.org). Neurological damage was reported in cats fed imported irradiated cat food, now banned by the Australian government, (for details go to www.Dr.FoxVet.com).

Chapter 7

Diets for Healthy Cats:
A Recipe for Disease?

W e have seen in the previous chapter that cats are very specialized obligatory carnivores. The evidence for this conclusion is inescapable. In fact, not even the pet food manufacturers dispute this, some even market their well-pet cat foods on the premise that their products better recognize the cat's uniquely carnivorous nature than do their competitors' products. While the pet food industry will argue that today's pet foods (all of them) are comprised of wholesome, completely nutritious ingredients, we have shown in this book that this is most certainly not the case. Pet food safety is only one issue that should concern pet owners. Even if the industry and the FDA could guarantee that pet foods would be free of toxins and of unwholesome, cheap ingredients, the formulas of these products would still, in many cases, be inadequate for maintaining the health of normal pets. This is because the nutrients that are provided to pets in commercial foods are dictated by the available economical ingredients that go into the foods, not the actual needs of the animals themselves. An industry based on the disposal of otherwise unusable byproducts of agriculture will formulate diets with a focus on what byproducts are actually available at any given time, and at what prices. Unfortunately, this means that pets eat what large companies decide they are willing to pay for, in a profit-driven industry. The pet's own biological needs are a decidedly secondary consideration.

So, we have the scraps of human food production being used to make up commercial pet food formulations, with vitamin/mineral supplements added in bulk to try to make these scrap-based foods complete and balanced for exclusive feeding of pets. This is not the best way to nourish any animal. Over the past twenty to thirty years, we have seen repeated examples of cats suffering harm from the exclusive feeding of commercial cat food. In the 1980s, a veterinary resident, Dr. Paul Pion, happened upon the discovery that the levels of an essential amino acid for the cat, taurine, were dangerously low in many commercial cat foods. This deficiency caused serious health problems, with many cats developing heart disease and going blind. Every one of the foods that were found to be taurine-deficient carried label claims that they were complete and balanced for the cat, and many of them even carried label claims that they had been proven to deliver this absolute level of nutrition using feeding trials.

Feeding Trials? What Feeding Trials?

If many of these foods had been shown to be complete and balanced using actual feeding trials, then how did this often fatal deficiency elude detection until it disabled and killed thousands of pet cats? The answer lies in the nature of the testing required for a food to qualify for the government's complete and balanced label guarantee.

The sad fact is that when a label states that the food in the can or bag has been tested and shown to be complete and balanced for feeding pets, that statement falsely leads the pet food purchaser to believe that the specific food they are purchasing has underdone some kind of rigorous test to make sure it has enough, but not too much, of any particular nutrient and that all of those nutrients are in balance with one another. The truth is, however, that the food consumers put in their shopping carts has, itself, never been tested at all. It is likely that even the formulation upon which the food is based has not been tested either. AAFCO rules are so lax and so unscientific that no food today is really tested in any nutritionally valid way. The few tests the pet food companies do conduct in order to appear to meet consumer expectations are done in only a handful of pets for an astonishingly brief period of time (six months or less). (See Appendix C).

In the case of the taurine deficiency that was caused by so many supposedly rigorously tested foods, the small amount of testing done on a pitifully few samples of those foods was far below the scientific standard needed to disclose such a horrifying deficiency. What is worse, nothing has changed in the testing requirements for pet foods in the two decades since Pion's discovery. Today, pet are just as vulnerable to these kinds of toxicities and deficiencies as they were then. Excesses of vitamin D supplementation in marketed pet foods have occurred and caused illness in pets since the taurine deficiency scandal, proving this point.

The Carbohydrate Debacle

Unfortunately, vitamins and minerals are not the only nutrients that appear in pet foods in improper amounts. For cats, the glut of highly processed carbohydrate and sugar in commercial foods is just as dangerous, and far more widespread. As we shall see when we discuss the many diseases caused by excesses of this nutrient, even a few years of feeding of high carbohydrate foods can lead to disastrous results for even the healthiest cat. We will discuss four of the most common of these nutritionally-caused diseases: obesity, diabetes, urinary tract disease (bladder problems and FUS, the feline urologic syndrome), and IBD (inflammatory bowel disease). But mention should be made first of two serious fat-related conditions, namely hepatic lipidosis, or fatty liver disease, and pancreatitis, two painful and potentially fatal conditions. Fatty liver disease can be triggered when a sick cat stops eating and the cat is fat from too many carbs in the diet. The stored body fat is flushed into the bloodstream a normal response to starvation but because there is so much, the liver becomes over-saturated. Too much fat in the diet can cause pancreatitis in dogs, an acute and painful inflammation of the pancreas. The causes of this condition in cats is less clearly defined, a high carb diet again being suspect. A low fat diet is called for in animals who succumb to pancreatitis that is often associated with diabetes in cats.

Feline Obesity

Many of today's pet cats are at least somewhat overweight, even obese. The typical well-cared for average-sized feline will weigh 13 to 14 pounds (a 25 percent increase in body weight over ideal), and a disturbing number will even tip the scales at a whopping, morbidly obese 20 pounds plus. What is as alarming as the epidemic of obesity itself is the fact that few of these cats' owners understand how seriously ill their beloved pets really are.

The reason so many attentive owners don't know that their cats are fat is simple; it has been decades since they have even seen a cat that has that natural sleek, athletic build of the truly healthy mixed-breed cat. So what happened to the fit, swift, agile feline athletes we knew just a few decades ago? How did we turn millions of cats into the lethargic, overweight, food-obsessed couch-potatoes we see today?

Approximately twenty years ago, a quiet revolution in the family cat's lifestyle began in the U.S. At that time, many owners began to understand the growing dangers to their free-roaming pets from fast-moving automobiles in suburban and urban areas, as well as the increasing possibility of infectious disease spread from one free-roaming cat to another. To avoid these threats, owners began bringing, and keeping, their pet cats inside the home. This change greatly decreased the probability of early death due to disease or trauma, but new debilitating feline diseases became more and more common in middle-aged and older cats, obesity among them. The cat that had previously lived an athletic outdoor life, eating small prey animals, birds, and the occasional reptile or insect, was about to make a very big dietary change as the price of the safety of the indoor life.

Cat owners, like dog owners before them, have come to prefer the dry kibble form of food for their cats because of its convenience and seeming economy. The pet food industry has poured millions of dollars into marketing these dry foods because they are extremely cheap to make, and result in large profits for manufacturers. Without pet owners realizing it, the cat eating dry food was suddenly eating food more fit for herbivores, and getting a very wrong diet day in and day out. Instead of its natural meat-based diet, the dry-food-fed cat today eats a diet that would be better for a cow than a cat. Today's commercial dry cat foods, even those that are premium quality, are uniformly high in essentially pre-digested carbohydrate, an extremely unfit diet for any feline.

Dry Cat Foods Are Nutritionally Upside-Down

Consider that canned and dry forms of the exact same formula of any brand have very different energy nutrient profiles (energy nutrients are the protein, fat and carbohydrates of a food). Wet products have relatively high protein (usually about 40 to 55 percent of the dry matter if moisture is removed), moderate fat (usually 25 to 35 percent of dry matter) and low carbohydrate (usually about 2 to 8 percent dry matter), with fiber, vitamins and minerals making up the balance.

Dry foods, however, bear no nutritional resemblance to their corresponding wet versions. A dry food will usually have about 20 to 35 percent protein dry matter, 10 to 25 percent fat dry matter, and 25 to 50 percent carbohydrate dry matter, with the balance made up of fiber and vitamin/mineral mix. Dry foods often have relatively high fiber content (5 to 8 percent) while canned foods, unless they have fiber deliberately added as a separate ingredient, have almost no fiber. Why would different forms of the exact same formula have such very different energy nutrient content? Do kittens and cats have different needs depending on whether they are eating canned or dry?

The answer is no. The cat has the exact same energy nutrient needs (and tolerance) no matter what form of food it eats. So why are these formulas so different?

Pet Food Technology

The production of a dry kibble using the process of extrusion, (the same process used in making breakfast cereal and high carbohydrate snack foods) dictates the ingredients that will be used to make dry pet foods. Extrusion technology requires plenty of starch to form the light kibble (or human breakfast cereal and snack foods) that this process is known for. So, pet food companies add tons of corn, rice, wheat, oats, barley and other grains, the less expensive the better, to the meat meal and other low volume ingredients that make up dry pet foods. Recently, a dry food containing potato instead of cereal grain appeared on the market. But potato, like cereal grains, contains plenty of starchy carbohydrate.

Further compounding the problem, carbohydrate is predigested (broken down) by the extremes of cooking during extrusion, and this degraded starch enters the pet's bloodstream quickly as sugar. Nothing in the cat's evolutionary development could possibly have prepared it for a steady diet of this sugar-laden junk food.

In contrast, wet-formula cat foods do not require starch in their production. Puréed, chunked, sliced, or grilled meats go perfectly well into a sealed can or pouch that is then sterilized in a high-heat sterilizer. Wet foods have energy nutrient profiles that are high protein, low to moderate fat, and low carbohydrate, because this is the nutrient profile of meat-based food that will not be extruded.

Carbohydrates Cause Feline Obesity

Ask any pet food company scientist why they formulate such high levels of highly processed carbohydrate into their costliest dry cat foods, and they will insist that while the cat has no known requirement for carbohydrate, there is no known harm in using carbohydrate ingredients in cat food. They will further argue that those very ingredients allow production of the most marketable form of cat food, dry kibble.

Upsetting Appetite Signals

Further compounding the problem is the cat's unique system of signals from food that tell it that it is full and should stop eating. The cat evolved in an environment rich in protein and fat, but deficient in carbohydrate, so consumption of fat and protein evolved as the signal to the cat that it should cease intake when calorie needs are met. A high-carbohydrate diet has a minimal effect on intake signals in the cat, even as energy requirements are met and then exceeded. Not only is the cat's pancreas poorly suited to handling repetitive substantial sugar loads from highly processed dry cat food, the satiety system is also unable to respond to high carbohydrate intake by making the cat feel full.

The result of this dietary mismatch is cats that overeat highly processed-carbohydrate diets are stimulating repeated surges of insulin from their limited carnivore's pancreatic reserve. "They always seem to be hungry, their owners complain or else they see it as the cat loving the food so it must be good, otherwise they instinctively wouldn't eat it. Little wonder that many become overweight, even obese. Because most house cats are sexually altered, a physiologic state that reduces the cat's metabolic needs much as the attainment of middle age does in humans, the cycle becomes even more destructive and inescapable.

The observation that some cats somehow manage to escape becoming overweight on dry food diets is similar to the observation that not all humans who regularly eat junk and fast foods get overweight, become depressed, diabetic and have high blood pressure. They are the exceptions to the rule, individuals spared by good genes and a myriad of other, unknown, protective factors. We don't have tests to determine which cats have the good genes and which do not. What we do know is that dry kibbled cat food is a dangerous dietary choice for all cats, especially because there are superior, readily available alternatives.

Should We Be Concerned about Overweight Cats?

If your cat becomes seriously overweight, is this really a problem? Once a cat becomes greatly overweight, about 13 to 14 pounds and above for the average cat, many things change for that animal. Activity levels decrease, leading to even more weight gain. The cat loses its interest in and ability to groom itself, and the haircoat becomes dull and dry. Fecal residue at the rectum of the cat that cannot groom itself causes discomfort and even infection. Strain on joints causes many overweight cats to have pain when they jump, or just try to move quickly. The fat cat is a couch-potato, unwilling to play and interact with other animals or people, so quality of life deteriorates.

Low-Carb Transformation

One of the first of the many positive changes owners see when their cats change from a high-carb dry diet to a low-carb canned or raw one is an astonishing physical rejuvenation. Cats that have been couch potatoes begin to play with toys and chase around the house as if they were kittens again. They become far more interactive with the family than ever before. The cat does get more exercise, and that increased activity works together with the low-carb diet to reduce weight naturally. Further, cats on medication for arthritis can reduce or even stop medication altogether. Problems with constipation disappear; the dull dry coat is replaced by the lustrous healthy hair of the cat's younger days. The list of benefits goes on and on.

Prevention or correction of obesity in the cat is not merely an exercise in cosmetics, although the cat at its optimal weight is more beautiful, more agile and more graceful than the over-weight cat. Much more than that, helping our cats remain athletic and svelte helps them remain active and healthy for many more years of life. When a cat is living its life as nature intended it to do, at the weight its frame and structure were meant to maintain, all of its systems function at their best. The greatest threat to the cat's naturally healthful state is the present day practice of feeding dry commercial cat foods.

Diet Pet Foods Don't Work

If you have ever tried to reduce your overweight cat's excess pounds using one or more of the many weight-loss foods, you know they don't work. Why not? The answer is simple. Those new expensive foods are based upon the exact same faulty understanding of the cat that allowed the original foods to cause obesity in the first place. In developing the foods to correct the obesity caused by their regular foods, the pet food companies have not yet come to an understanding of the unique metabolic characteristics of the cat. Instead, they have simply applied tired old human dieting theory to their feline diet foods, perhaps in hopes that the rationale will be familiar and seem sensible to the humans who buy these foods for their cats.

Astonishingly, feline light or weight control foods are uniformly very low in fat, and this reduction in fat is compensated for with an increase in processed carbohydrate plus indigestible fiber. Such a diet cannot hope to reverse the damage done by the cat's previous, high carbohydrate diet. On this new diet, the cat receives even less natural nourishment because the added fiber creates constipating residue and decreases nutrient digestibility. The cat experiences even less satisfaction from protein and fat signals to its brain and craves more food. The increase in highly processed carbohydrate stimulates even greater overproduction

Is Your Cat Overweight?

If your cat is an adult female, she should weigh between 7 and 11 pounds at the most. Exceptions are pure-bred cats of the Maine Coon, Norwegian Forest Cat and Ragdoll breeds. Females of these breeds can weigh as much as 12 to 14 pounds.

If your cat is an adult male, and not one of the larger breed cats mentioned above, he should weigh 9 to 12 pounds at most. Males of the large breeds can weigh 13 to 18 pounds normally.

Even if your cat does not exceed the guidelines above, he or she may still be overweight. One way to tell is too stand your cat up on its back legs. Do you see a waist just below the ribcage and just above the hind legs? Cats should not be perfect rectangles or squares. They are designed to have shoulders and ribs that are broader than their hips, like an athletic human swimmer.

Another measure of a cat's degree of overweight is the fat under the skin over the ribs. If you place the palm of your hand against your cat's ribcage and can't feel ribs readily against your palm, then your cat is at least a little overweight. If you can't feel ribs even if you use your finger tips to feel for ribs, than your cat has a lot of fat under the skin there and is badly in need of a weight loss program.

If your cat doesn't groom itself anymore, or can't groom areas such as under its tail, hind legs and belly because of excess fat getting in the way, it's time for action to make your cat healthy again!

of insulin with deposition of more fat. The cycle continues. Usually, the cat does not lose weight unless portions are reduced to near-starvation levels. Arguably, this is a form of animal abuse; such cruel mistreatment for a manmade condition (feline obesity) is unethical and medically unacceptable.

Upsetting the Pancreas

Research into the causes and management of feline type 2 diabetes, including work originated by coauthor Elizabeth Hodgkins, and later verified by colleagues at one of these large companies, suggested strongly that the blood sugar level of the cat is rapidly influenced by the energy nutrients in its diet. Sugar from highly processed cereal grains in the dry diet floods the blood that carries nutrients from the digestive system to the liver, causing an alarm to go out to the pancreas. One of the most important jobs of this small organ near the cat's stomach is to keep the blood sugar level in the cat from rising to harmful levels. The pancreas produces and secretes insulin, a hormone that drives blood sugar into the cells of the body, thereby lowering the level of circulating sugar to more normal levels.

The normal cat pancreas tries to control this unnatural state by putting high levels of insulin into constant circulation. This high insulin level causes the accumulation of fat in the body as energy nutrients are driven into the cells, even in the absence of a need for all that energy. As high insulin levels succeed in lowering the blood sugar, the animal may even experience a relative hypoglycemia, or lower-than-normal blood sugar, which will trigger hunger and the additional consumption of high sugar dry food. A vicious cycle starts. Many humans can experience this rollercoaster of high and low blood glucose when they eat highly processed carbohydrate diets as well.

Feline Diabetes Epidemic

In 1990, experts estimated that the number of diabetic cats in the United States was at least 150,000 at any one time. Since then, the sheer numbers of pet cats have grown tremendously, and the negative influences causing this very serious disease have increased. Most veterinarians agree that they are seeing more and more feline diabetic patients as time goes by. This is an astounding number of cats to be affected simultaneously by a very serious, often fatal disease.

Some will say that this increase in numbers of diagnosed diabetics is not only due to the increase in cats overall, but also to the increased health care that today's cats receive. Even if an increase in the quantity of health care pet owners give their cats were a partial explanation, though, feline lifestyle changes during the past twenty-five years have also increased the chance that any cat will develop adult-onset diabetes in its lifetime.

We have discussed some of the lifestyle pressures that the indoor cat feels in the section about feline obesity. We know the indoor cat gets a bit less exercise than an outdoor cat. Exercise is important in preventing both obesity and diabetes in humans and this is probably true for cats as well. Even outdoor cats sleep a great deal, however, about eighteen to twenty hours per day. Play and hunting activities take up only a short period in even the free-roaming cat's daily schedule. Further, even indoor cats with little opportunity or need for strenuous exercise do not become obese when fed wet foods with little processed carbohydrate. The level of exercise restriction that an indoor cat experiences is not a critical factor in development of either obesity or diabetes, despite current thinking that this is the sole reason for these problems.

The Insulin Fix and Alternatives

Adult-onset diabetes in the cat (type 2 diabetes), is caused when there is a release of large amounts of glucose (blood sugar) into the bloodstream without the pancreas making and releasing enough insulin to handle that sugar. In diabetics, the pancreas does not respond to rising blood sugar. When this happens, the cat begins to feel great thirst and will produce much more urine than usual. Usually, a diabetic cat's appetite also increases, but it will still lose weight over time. As the disease progresses without treatment, the cat will start to vomit, become very dehydrated, and act very sick.

The diagnosis of feline diabetes is generally easy. Blood and urine tests which show significantly elevated sugar levels accompanied by the typical clinical signs are sufficient, although other tests will show how much secondary damage is present as well. Because the diabetic cat lacks enough insulin of its own making, treatment after diagnosis consists of insulin injections under the skin, just as it does for human diabetics. For decades, this has been the standard approach to treating feline diabetes. For decades, most cats have not done well after their diagnosis, even when their owners have been devoted to giving them good care and daily insulin shots.

The High Fiber Fix Failure

In the 1980s, researchers studied how diet might be used to improve the quality of life for diabetic cats. They concluded that combining high fiber with a cat's normal diet would help control diabetes in cats. This high-fiber idea became popular with veterinarians, and pet food manufacturers who funded the research started making diets that had a lot of added indigestible fiber in the form of cellulose.

The theory was that the fiber in the diet would interfere with the absorption of dietary sugar from the intestines into the bloodstream. With this decrease in digestibility, dietary sugar would enter the bloodstream more slowly and would not cause the wide swings of blood sugar that make controlling the diabetic cat so difficult. This theory seemed logical. The diets have been prescribed by every veterinarian in small animal practice for the treatment of feline diabetes for two decades now. There is just one problem: They don't work.

Unfortunately, the high-fiber diet research compared diets with high carbohydrate and fiber to diets with high carbohydrate without fiber. In this experiment, the high carbohydrate diet with the high fiber did seem to provide more control than the high carbohydrate diet without fiber. Despite this, the conclusion from this study that high-carbohydrate/high-fiber diets were the best dietary approach for controlling feline diabetes is misleading.

The researchers of the 1980s did not study how low-carbohydrate diets affect feline diabetics. Had they done so, they would have discovered that taking the carbohydrate (sugar) out of the diet is a far greater help in the control of feline diabetes than adding indigestible vegetable residue to high-sugar diets.

An Important Discovery

In 1994, coauthor Hodgkins began the research that led to the discovery of the critical importance of diet in the management of feline diabetes. Her cat, Punkin, developed diabetes while consuming premium dry cat food. Like so many cats with diabetes, Punkin was very hard to regulate. His blood glucose would swing from very high to very low. He suffered episodes of an extremely serious condition called diabetic ketoacidosis, which happens to a cat when too little insulin leads to prolonged high blood sugar levels.

Punkin also had episodes of hypoglycemia (blood sugar too low) leading to seizures. His case was a medical nightmare. After suffering with Punkin's disease for a year, Hodgkins became so frustrated that she did something that no one had done before that time. She asked the questions: Why is this so hard?" "What are veterinarians and owners doing that is keeping cats like Punkin from getting better?

Having worked in the pet food industry for many years, Hodgkins knew that to make dry cat foods a manufacturer had to use lots of cereal, just like breakfast cereal makers do. She knew that dry kibbled foods are very high in refined carbohydrates and simple sugar in the bag. Making things worse, when today's cat grazes on high carbohydrate food all day, this assault goes on and on. This is true of the high-carbohydrate, high-fiber diets just as it is true of the high-carbohydrate, low-fiber diets.

Hodgkins wondered if his high-carbohydrate diet was making Punkin's diabetes hard to control. Could the food Punkin was eating have too much carbohydrate and simple sugar and too little of the other nutrients Punkin needed to be healthy and control his diabetes? Hodgkins changed her cat's diet from one of the high-carbohydrate, high-fiber dry foods to one of the canned, high -protein, low-carbohydrate kitten foods on the market. As a result, Punkin's blood sugar levels fell immediately after only one day on the canned diet. Within five days on the new diet, Punkin didn't need any insulin injections at all. He had good blood sugar levels just by eating the canned kitten food alone.

But Punkin was only one cat, so this experiment would need to be extended to other diabetic cats to be sure of the results. In a short time, many more diabetic cats were switched from dry, high-fiber diets to canned, low-carbohydrate diets. All of the cats improved dramatically. Many, like Punkin, went off insulin shots altogether. This was a huge step forward for cats with diabetes and their owners.

What Causes Diabetes in the Cat?

For many years, veterinarians have known that obesity in cats seemed to make the obese patient more likely to get diabetes. In fact, most of us thought that being overweight actually caused diabetes. Today, it seems unlikely that excess pounds in a cat are a cause of this condition. Obesity in the cat and feline diabetes may well have the same parent causes, but they are not a direct cause of one another. Although we do see many feline diabetics that are also quite overweight, these cats are probably genetically predisposed to get both of these problems from the same root causes. We often see cats that have one, but not both, of these conditions; this is undoubtedly because of each cat's unique genetic make-up. The significant numbers of always-slender cats that have full-blown diabetes suggest that being the proper weight does not protect a cat from this disease. Also, we see very overweight cats that become diabetic, but then recover from their diabetes easily on proper diet and insulin, long before they lose the weight they need to lose.

Organs Harmed

Because today's indoor cat is almost always eating dry cat food, with its extremely high sugar content, a cat with any genetic tendency to become obese and/or become diabetic will do just that when sugar (in the form of processed dietary carbohydrate) is a large part of its diet. The onset of obesity and diabetes is triggered by constant flooding of the cat's system with refined carbohydrate from the dry diet, day after day, month after month, and year after year. This steady sugar rush finally exhausts the small pancreatic capabilities of the carnivore. In many cats, relentless sugar surges cause the pancreas to turn that sugar to fat. Obesity, with or without diabetes, follows.

The pancreas is not the only organ system affected in the dry-food-fed cat, however. When the cat's diet is high in carbohydrate and sugar, the function of the animal's liver also becomes abnormal. Instead of responding to small drops in blood sugar levels by releasing stored glucose, the liver in the dry-food-fed cat fails to respond. The constant high dietary sugar load has caused the liver to lose some of its ability to react quickly to falling blood sugar levels. Thus, in the dry-food-fed cat, the pancreas cannot respond to high sugar any more, and the liver cannot respond to low sugar. The cat has become a complete carbohydrate cripple. This crippled cat is completely dependent upon exactly the right amount of insulin from the outside. It is extremely difficult to provide such precise amounts of injected insulin. This is why owners find it extremely frustrating to try to manage the dry-food-fed cat.

Why Low-Carbohydrate Diets Work So Well

It was not a surprise that cats eating foods with a lot less sugar would have lower blood sugar levels (just like human diabetics who do not eat candy or other high sugar foods), but it was a bit surprising that so many of them would stop needing insulin shots. Up to that time, veterinarians had always thought that a diabetic cat's pancreas had stopped doing its job forever. It was certain that in Hodgkins' test cats, the pancreas had started to work again, otherwise they would have continued to need the insulin injections, at least at low doses. This was very exciting; it meant that many diabetics, maybe almost all of them, can actually be cured of this disease.

Feline Bladder Disease

For many years, veterinarians have struggled to manage several related diseases of the urinary tract of their feline patients, with very limited success. The typically affected cat strains to urinate, may have blood in its urine, and can even become blocked and unable to urinate at all. This becomes a life-threatening emergency situation that requires immediate veterinary attention. Chronic, painful bladder conditions often lead to cats becoming house-soilers, for which they may be mistakenly disciplined for being disobedient, or are thrown out, and even euthanized.

Why Do Cats Develop Urinary Tract Problems?

Cats are a very successful and naturally healthy species. Left to themselves, cats in general do not have major urinary tract problems. Yet, in the 1970s and 1980s, veterinarians began to see very large numbers of cases of that were generally lumped under the label of feline urologic syndrome, or FUS, that could include cystitis (bladder inflammation and infection), bladder crystal and stone formation, and urinary blockage in their feline patients. We refer to this syndrome as UTI, urinary tract inflammation. Many cats died when their blockages caused acute renal failure and treatment arrived too late. Veterinary surgeons even developed a new surgical procedure, called a perineal urethrostomy, in which the male cat's urethra is amputated to better allow urine with crystals to flow from the bladder to the outside. Unfortunately, this surgery and other less drastic medical treatments were not always effective long-term.

The Magnesium Crystal and Ash Myth

The analysis the experts applied to this problem at that time was flawed, and the solution faulty. The rise of urinary tract diseases in the cat coincided exactly with the increasing use of dry kibble diets for cats Scientists at the pet food companies studied the problem and concluded that it was the magnesium in commercial pet foods that caused UTI. They concluded this simply because the most common type of crystals formed in affected cats was composed of a magnesium compound.

The experts reasoned that the amount of magnesium in the foods of affected cats must be too high, causing magnesium levels in the urine to be too high. Their theory went that high magnesium in the urine caused stones to form in the bladder. The experts failed to consider that the natural prey diet of cats also contained significant magnesium but was composed of entirely different types of ingredients. Regardless, cat owners were soon buying low ash content cat foods, the popular term for special cat foods low in magnesium.

The pet food scientists did notice a key difference in the urine of dry-food-fed cats. The urine of such cats was alkaline in its pH, rather than acid. Magnesium crystals form in alkaline urine, not acid urine. They reasoned that if they added acid to the food of these cats and removed the magnesium, the problem would go away. Many different prescription-type foods appeared on the market and were available through veterinarians as treatment or prevention of UTI. This approach was only partially successful, however. Many cats with UTI that were managed with these diets still had recurrences of their disease. Worse, some of them developed a different type of crystals, made of a calcium salt, because their urine had become too acidic. For these cats, the cure was as devastating as the original disease. They developed calcium oxalate crystals in their urinary bladders, and so their suffering continued and intensified, since the experts knew of no cure, except surgery in extreme cases.

Lack of Water

Another reason dry food causes UTI is because of its very low moisture content compared to wet foods. Cats that eat dry diets and have access to plenty of fresh water will still have consistently more concentrated urine than those that eat wet foods. Although dry-food-fed cats drink extra water, they do not make up for the lower moisture of their food by drinking enough free water. This situation is most likely the result of the cat's evolutionary origins in the desert and other types of arid environments. The cat's thirst drive for non-dietary water is not strong. It never needed to be strong when the animal was eating high-moisture foods. When we deprive the cat of dietary water, we invariably cause a state of relative dehydration, with disastrous results.

Surprisingly, the studies the pet food companies conducted to find a cat food that would eliminate the UTI problem never included a low carbohydrate, meat-based wet food as one of the options they studied, despite evidence that the dry form of food as well as high starch (from cereal in dry formulas) were two important factors in this disease. The test diets in these studies were usually low-moisture, carbohydrate-based foods with different kinds of acidifying ingredients and different levels of magnesium. The role of high levels of highly processed carbohydrate in dry form was never questioned in the nutritional research into this disease.

Rather than adding strong acids to disease-causing commercial dry diets, the better solution would have been to develop high-moisture diets based on the natural nutrient profile of the cat's evolutionary diet. Not surprisingly, adding artificial acidifiers to commercial cat foods has been a disaster for cats.

The Ultimate Cure

Ironically, the means to eradicate UTI from the feline population has always been right in front of us. Plant-based cat foods, specifically dry cat foods with their very high amounts of processed cereal and very low moisture content, cause UTI, pure and simple. Even the special, acid-containing foods for UTI cats can, and do, continue to promote this terrible condition. On the other hand, cats eating meat-based wet foods simply do not develop UTI. The problem is not, and has never been, the level of magnesium in the diet of UTI cats. The problem is the extremely low-moisture, alkaline-urine-producing, high-processed-carbohydrate formulas of dry cat foods.

Inflammatory Bowel Disease/ Inflammatory Bowel Syndrome

Today, chronic gastrointestinal disease in adult cats, characterized by recurrent diarrhea, is commonplace. It is another reason cats become house-soilers and mess around their litter boxes, leading to their being punished, even abandoned. Despite this epidemic, no relevant clinical research has been conducted to study the nature and causes of IBD/IBS in felines. Affected patients often undergo extensive, expensive medical work-ups, including biopsy of their gastrointestinal tracts, with the final determination that they have IBD (inflammatory bowel disease) or IBS (inflammatory bowel syndrome). Unfortunately, subsequent treatment is often less than successful. Fortunately, there is a simple explanation and solution in the majority of these cases.

What Is IBD?

Inflammatory bowel disease, or inflammatory bowel syndrome is a pathologist's description of very general processes occurring in the tissues of the cat's digestive tract. These terms do not really tell us anything about the underlying cause of those processes. What is clear is that in cats with this problem the tissues of the intestines, and sometimes the stomach, are involved in a chronic (long-term) immune system stimulation that disrupts normal digestive functions. During inflammation, fluids are secreted into the intestines resulting in diarrhea. Excessive motility in the inflamed tissues adds to this problem, and also decreases the assimilation of nutrients from food. If the stomach is involved, the cat vomits as well.

Because IBD is a disease of immune reaction, we assume that some immune system stimulation in the digestive or gastro-intestinal (GI) tract is causing this reaction. Most experts agree on this point. Food is by far the most likely stimulant of this allergic reaction because the ingredients in the cat's food are the major substances that contact the surface of the stomach and intestines. Proteins and other molecules in the diet cause the surface of the GI tract to react as though those molecules were foreign invaders. To solve the problem, it is logical that we need to change the kinds of substances that the cat's GI organs have to process.

How Is IBD Treated?

Up to now, IBD has been treated with immune system-suppressing drugs like prednisone and so-called hypoallergenic diets. This idea is logical because IBD is a immune-reactive condition, but the results are seldom if ever, highly satisfactory. The immune-suppressing drugs have side effects, and most of the commercial hypoallergenic diets are far from hypoallergenic. These commercial diets attempt to use novel protein source ingredients, like lamb and rice, to achieve the desired results. Unfortunately, the form of diet used is almost always dry. The reality is that the cat with IBD is reacting to many of the highly unnatural ingredients in the commercial food, especially the dry form of the food.

Everything about dry commercial foods, and even most commercial wet foods, is capable of causing an allergic reaction in the cat. There is nothing about the ingredients or formulation of dry cat foods that make them suitable for the cat. It makes little difference whether the protein sources of such foods come from chicken, beef, lamb, fish, soy, glutens or any other protein ingredients. If the cat

HOW PLANT-BASED CAT FOODS CAUSE
URINARY TRACT DISEASE

Because predators like the cat consume plenty of bone along with meat, the metabolites of the carnivorous diet include lots of minerals, including magnesium. Magnesium in the cat's diet is not, and never was, the problem. The problem is dry cat foods because:

• Dry cat foods, with their high plant content, cause a very alkaline urine pH. This is an unnatural environment in the cat's bladder, leading to inflammation. The consumption of meat causes an acid pH in the bladder. This is the normal, healthy environment.

• Dry cat foods provide almost no moisture, while a natural prey diet provides 75 to 80 percent moisture. The cat has a low thirst-drive to consume free water because of its evolutionary origins. Thus, the dry-food-fed cat is usually sub-clinically dehydrated, and its urine is very concentrated. This unnaturally high concentration of minerals and other constituents in the urine, along with an alkaline pH, leads to UTI.

When a cat consumes a wet, meat-based diet, the resulting urine has a natural acid pH and is more diluted than the urine of dry-food-fed cats. These conditions do not allow the formation of crystals and stones, and eliminate the inflammation that characterizes idiopathic cystitis.

with IBD doesn't react to the protein ingredients, it can and almost always will react to the dozens of other ingredients in combination with those proteins.

Hypoallergenic-Hyped Diets

In recent years, some pet food manufacturers have developed second-generation hypoallergenic foods. In these very expensive cat foods, all of the protein has been broken down to amino acids, the basic components of protein. The theory behind these foods is that if you reduce dietary protein to its basic amino acids, you would have the ultimate novel protein. Unfortunately, this approach does not work well in the cat itself. These diets have many of the same limitations and abnormal formulation characteristics that normal cat foods do. Because the pet food company formulators do not understand the basic problem with all commercial dry foods, and those wet foods with ingredients that are abnormal in the diet of the cat, they have ignored the most obvious solution.

The ingredients used in commercial pet foods aren't really hypoallergenic to the majority of patients. These ingredients are processed in industrial plants that produce dozens of other products with very different ingredients.

Cross-contamination between hypoallergenic and non-hypoallergenic products is a very real problem. The number of steps, the number of machines, and the number of hands that are required to produce the hypoallergenic diets make it all but impossible for these kinds of diets to deliver the results they promise. As we have already discussed, however, there is no scientific evaluation of the effectiveness of these diets compared with more simple, less processed foods, so their failure remains a shadowy secret.

Because the diet change that would have entirely solved the problem of inflammatory bowel disease has never been recognized by those making pet foods for cats, the right way to correct the problem has never been used in most commercial cat foods prescribed for the IBD cat. There is a small number of canned commercial foods that do not contain high-carbohydrate ingredients. These can be helpful in mild cases of IBD if they are used early in the allergic process. These hypoallergenic canned foods do not resolve more severe cases, however. In such cases, the best solution for this problem is to go back to the basics of the cat's natural diet. Cats with IBD are especially sensitive to the artificiality and over-processed nature of commercial foods; they need their proper fuel to run well. Because of this, a meat-based homemade diet can be lifesaving.

Feeding Raw Meat to Your Cat:
Is It Safe and Sensible?

Today, many veterinary nutrition experts advise against feeding homemade meat diets to pets, without any qualification. This rigid view ignores the simple fact that the cat we enjoy as a pet today developed as a highly successful and prolific species on that very diet over millennia of time. There should be no unqualified bias against feeding raw meat to the obligatory carnivore that is the cat, perched as it is atop the food chain with its top-predator brethren. Day in, day out, month in, month out, for thousands of years before Western civilization saw light of day, the close ancestors of the cat caught and ate meat, and those ancestors ate it raw.

What About Contamination?

Typically, raw meat remains frozen until immediately before feeding. All of the logical precautions against bacterial contamination that we observe in handling meat for our families apply to the practice of feeding this meat to our cats. While many will argue that these precautions are not entirely foolproof, a review of available documentation of diet-caused illness in pets shows that far more disease is caused by commercial foods than any type of homemade diets. The evolution of the cat has prepared it for the consumption of low levels of bacteria with its food. It is unimaginable that an animal that hunts, kills prey, and then eats that prey off the ground, sometimes hours or even days after the kill, is not capable naturally of resisting food poisoning of the type that most critics of raw meat feeding are concerned about. The notion that only commercial pet food producers can nourish our cats properly, after all these years of evolution before there were commercial pet foods, is just plain stupid.

We live at a time when human nutritionists insist that healthful diets must include unprocessed fresh, whole foods to establish and maintain health. At the same time, we see frightening examples of how unsafe commercial pet food products can be under some circumstances, as described in Chapter 2. Despite all this, many experts continue to hold fast to the idea that our cats (and dogs) must eat commercial products that are far less fresh and whole than raw meat, and are clearly not safer from contamination. Dry cat foods, full of processed carbohydrates and sugar and coated with fat and fermented liquids from animal entrails, sits on the shelf, exposed to air, for weeks, months or more. How can anyone believe that such a food is likely to be free of contamination? This is completely illogical, and nothing more than a bad habit that must be broken.

What About Nutrition?

Many experts are adamant that homemade meat-based diets will inevitably be nutritionally inadequate. They argue that commercial pet foods are complete and balanced for all life stages, or certain stages, as certified by feeding trials outlined by the American Association of Feed Control Officials (AAFCO). They insist that raw meat diets, with or without supplements, are not so tested, and so cannot be trusted to be good nutrition for pets.

The problems with this argument are many. We have discussed previously the problems with the AAFCO feeding trials, and how these trials have failed to disclose serious, even fatal, nutritional inadequacies in commercial pet foods in the past. Veterinarians and experts who believe that the adequacy testing done on commercial pet foods meets even minimal scientific standards are mistaken, as we have documented in Chapter 5. In reality, no food raw meat, or commercial canned or dry has been rigorously tested in long-term feeding studies prior to use in pets. In that regard, commercial foods have no advantage over homemade ones.

The long-term feeding trials needed to establish the safety and adequacy of pet foods have, ironically and tragically, been conducted in owned pets after the owners of those pets purchased the foods to feed their pets. The feeding trials for commercial cat foods, particularly dry cat foods, are terrible failures in which the test subjects (our own pets) are suffering from obesity, diabetes, urinary tract disease, IBD, and many other allergic conditions, to name a few of those conditions we know about. Had these foods been tested prior to release for sale, as they should have been, they would not have passed those tests.

Raw Meat Diets and Health Issues

How are raw meat diets doing in their feeding trials? Raw meat diets, properly designed, are proving considerably more nutritionally complete and balanced than their commercial rivals. (See Chapter 9.) Owners who feed high-protein, low-carbohydrate meat-based diets, including homemade diets, see far less obesity, diabetes, urinary tract disease, or IBD than those who feed dry commercial foods. Their cats are livelier, seem happier, and are sleek and shiny. Further, nutritional deficiencies in cats fed well-designed homemade diets are non-existent. If people are capable of properly feeding their own families, they are certainly capable of feeding their pets without resorting to opening a bag or can of processed food to do it.

The Definitive Treatment for IBD/IBS

Cats with even the most intractable and long-standing IBD will respond extremely well to raw ground rabbit meat as a starting diet. The change in such a cat is almost beyond imagining. The solution to the problem, as is the case with other nutritionally caused feline diseases, is simple and easy to understand.

A Call to Action

It is clearly time for pet owners and their veterinarians to begin thinking for themselves. Despite the glut of pet food marketing that blankets our everyday lives, we can no longer indulge the luxury of trusting blindly those packaged messages. The federal government and the pet food industry have failed us and our pets, that much is clear. Now, it is up to each of us to assume that failed responsibility and learn what we need to know to care for our pets, relying on our own intelligence and common sense to get this right for their sake!

Chapter 8

When Cat Foods Become Drugs: A Prescription for Disaster

We have discussed in preceding chapters the problems associated with feeding of commercial cat foods to healthy pets. We have even shown how many such foods can cause disease. The reader may naturally wonder, in light of this information about nutritionally caused diseases, about the usefulness and safety of the many different prescription-type foods that are commonly prescribed for treating many feline disease conditions. This topic is discussed in Chapter 5, but calls for another take, especially from the cat's perspective.

Prescription-Type Diets Are Essentially Drugs

If you think about it, the special commercial foods that many veterinarians utilize to manage feline disease are really drugs under the definition of drug contained in the Federal Food Drug and Cosmetic Act (FFDCA), the law that governs the regulation of prescription medications and foods for both humans and animals in the United States. The FFDCA defines drugs as articles intended for use in the diagnosis, cure, mitigation, treatment, or prevention of disease in man or other animals. Clearly, the foods that certain manufacturers market to veterinarians and their clients as part of the management of various medical conditions in pets fall under this definition. Undeniably, the very reason these foods exist, and the entire focus of their marketing to veterinary practitioners, is the treatment of disease conditions. It is ironic that many of the problems these foods are purported to treat have been caused by the so-called wellness diets made by the very same companies!

The FFDCA has very specific guidelines for any claims a manufacturer makes that a particular food has benefits in the treatment of disease. These rules require that the scientific community evaluate study data and determine that there is sufficient evidence that such claims are valid and that their appearance on any food or supplement label is not misleading to the average consumer of that product. A small exception to these stringent requirements is provided for nutritional supplements that bear the disclaimer on the label that product claims …have not been evaluated by the Food and Drug Administration. This product is not intended to diagnose, treat, cure, or prevent any disease.

Thus we see that the regulations that are supposed to regulate drugs, foods, and supplements used as drugs by medical professionals, require that these substances must be proven safe and effective before they are marketed as therapeutic agents, or that they bear a disclaimer notifying the consumer that no tests have been done. We would expect pet food to fit into one of these categories, but the sad fact is that prescription-type pet foods neither undergo testing nor bear the disclaimer that they are untested. How can this possibly be?

Certainly, pharmaceutical companies must spend many millions of dollars and many years establishing adequate safety and efficacy data for their new pharmaceuticals. Nothing like this kind of scientific testing is conducted before a therapeutic (prescription-type) pet food goes to market and is fed to millions of cats and dogs, even though the very same laws govern both types of drugs. Although the federal Food and Drug Administration (FDA) has the same kind of responsibility to regulate pet foods that it has to regulate human drugs and supplements, this agency has essentially defaulted on that responsibility, leaving pet owners up there without a net. As a practical matter, the FDA is stretched very thin just trying to keep up with the human drug and food regulations. This agency simply has no resources for enforcing the FFDCA upon pet foods in this country. As much as it is unfair to consumers that there is no effective regulation of pet foods and the bold, broad claims made on their labels and in their marketing programs, the sad reality is that the pet food industry presently does as it pleases with no effective regulatory oversight.

As we discussed in the previous chapter, the only real testing that occurs in the case of pet foods, even the prescription-type used to manage disease in pets, is the real-life feeding of those untested foods to peoples' pets. This is, of course, an outrageous situation; what owner would agree to pay high prices for medical-management products (actual drugs or foods used as drugs) for their pet if the safety and efficacy of that regimen were going to be determined by the results of using those products on their pet? In human medicine, when drugs or devices are tested in final stage clinical trials on human patients in order to collect critical safety and efficacy data prior to FDA approval, those patients are always informed that they are participating in clinical trials. Each patient must consent to participate in the trial (called informed consent). In exchange for their consent, patients in these clinical trials receive their treatment at no charge.

There should be regulated clinical trials prior to marketing of a new prescription-type food, with informed consent from the pet owner, and relief from charge for the test food and monitoring of the results of the test. Those veterinarians who place their feline (and canine) patients into the current unofficial clinical trials of therapeutic foods are completely unaware that they are doing so. Pet food companies assure veterinarians that these foods have already undergone rigorous testing for safety and effectiveness in the disease for which they are labeled. Veterinary clinicians do not receive notice of potential adverse reactions to watch for from use of the food, because such information is not yet available. The practitioner does not expect or look for adverse effects, because there has been no warning about such effects. Reactions that do occur are attributed erroneously to some peculiarity of the pet, not the food. As a result, even though there is a clinical trial underway, albeit on owned pets whose owners pay to be in the trial, no results pointing to problems with the test food are ever generated, and unsafe products continue to be prescribed to countless pets for decades.

Feline Urinary Tract Disease Prescription Diets

One of the best examples, although certainly not the only one, of this appalling state of affairs is the widespread use of acidifying diets to treat feline bladder problems. For thirty years, an epidemic of feline urinary tract disease, usually related to the formation of a type of crystal or stone on the urinary bladder (often referred to as urinary tract inflammation or UTI), has plagued cats eating commercial cat foods, especially dry cat foods as discussed in the previous chapter. Most of the early cases of UTI were characterized by urine with a very alkaline pH from the digestion of vegetable matter in the commercial foods. The alkalinity of the urine contributed to the development of crystals and stones in the bladder.

One of the major pet food companies, Hill's Pet Nutrition, developed a special diet that contained large amounts of acid to counteract the alkalinizing effects of the poor quality ingredients in cat foods. They marketed this food as a therapeutic diet, available to veterinarians only, for cats with UTI. Even though the diet did not eliminate the problem, the massive marketing of the company convinced veterinarians and owners alike that the special diet was the best way to deal with this very serious disease. Ironically, many of the cats on this special acidifying diet developed a new type of disease, also characterized by crystal and stone formation, but the crystals and stones were of a different type. The precipitates found in the original disease were made up primarily of magnesium; these new precipitates were made up predominantly of calcium. Calcium precipitates in acid urine. The new therapeutic diet was, in fact, causing a disease as fearful as the one it was supposed to manage!

How was it possible for a major pet food company to market a therapeutic diet that actually caused a new disabling medical disease for so many decades without anyone suspecting? This travesty came about because this life-threatening adverse reaction was never discovered in the way adverse reactions to human drugs and devices are discovered, in clinical trials conducted prior to market approval. Even though this therapeutic diet was available only on the prescription of a veterinarian, just as prescription drugs are, there were no pre-marketing clinical trials, no documentation of adverse effects of the diet, no approval process by the FDA, and no notification to veterinarians about this adverse effect. Unmonitored clinical trials were carried on for decades on sick pets with no one the wiser.

Remarkably, this same company has recently introduced a new therapeutic diet that is supposed to treat magnesium-related disease without causing calcium-related disease. Apparently, the company has slowly but surely realized that there was a terrible problem with the original acidifying diet products. However, before we become too relieved that there has finally been some corrective action to fix the defect in the first of these foods, we should realize that this new diet rests upon no more scientific testing than the original diet did. In fact, this new diet may cause an altogether new set of problems that will only be discovered after thousands, maybe hundreds of thousands, of cats are sickened by its untested formula before anyone notices.

Hill's is not the only company that has created these kinds of problems. Several years after the original therapeutic diet became widely used in managing UTI in cats, many other companies developed their own versions of this kind of diet. Today, there are dozens of such products, and even most well-cat maintenance diets today contain untested amounts of powerful acidifying agents.

For the past twenty-five years, no additional progress has been made in dealing with UTI in cats. Veterinarians and cat owners have resigned themselves to the existence of this common and very serious problem, with nothing available to prevent it or cure it satisfactorily. Although the numbers of cats that must have the painful and mutilating surgery for UTI (see Chapter 7) have decreased, this surgery is still recommended for many cats that continue to relapse on their diets of expensive prescription-type dry cat foods. Many of these cats are diagnosed with a form of UTI called idiopathic cystitis, which means bladder inflammation with no known cause. Veterinarians reason that if the special diets cannot control the problem, then the cause must be complex and mysterious, beyond understanding and solution.

Feline Diabetes Diets

The first prescription-type diabetes diets for cats, initially marketed several decades ago, were not based on any valid scientific research, but rather very simplistic comparisons of high carbohydrate commercial maintenance formulas with formulas that contained significant amounts of added indigestible fiber. These first studies, sponsored by the manufacturer of the test diets, concluded erroneously that high carbohydrate, high-fiber diets were optimum for managing the diabetic cat. No additional, truly objective studies were ever done, and for decades, countless feline diabetics struggled hopelessly with their disease while consuming the very kind of food that had caused their diabetes in the first place.

Finally, in 2001, one of the largest pet food companies, Ralston Purina (now Nestlé Purina), introduced the first truly effective low carbohydrate canned cat food for the management of feline diabetes. This formula is based on the work described in the U.S. patent 6,203,825 and the publications that came out of that same work. This food works remarkably well to reduce the insulin dependency of diabetic cats. There is nothing magical about this product, however. It is based on the simple principle that cats are obligatory carnivores and have very specific requirements for nutrients as a result of their carnivore's metabolism. Based on meat, this first truly effective diabetes diet was nothing more than a return to the natural dietary composition of the cat. Because of this, any canned or raw diet that provides nutrients from meat will have this same kind of efficacy in the management and reversal of feline diabetes.

Unfortunately, the story of this first truly effective method for dietary management of feline disease does not end with the introduction of this meat-based canned product. The developing company apparently did not understand that the reason this food was effective was its low sugar/starch content. Further, the market demand for dry form pet foods, and the profitability of dry cat foods, apparently made it impossible for Purina to forgo having a dry cat food version of the original canned diabetes management (DM) diet, regardless of effectiveness. A dry form of DM was formulated, without any efficacy testing and comparison with the canned version of DM, and introduced to the market as identical to the successful earlier version. Other companies did the same, and today, there are a number of dry DM diets for cats that are as harmful to cats as the maintenance dry foods that cause feline diabetes in the first place. They are not appropriate nutrition for any cat, diabetic or otherwise, because their nutrient profiles are dictated by extrusion technology, not feline nutrition. Without scientific evaluation and government oversight of food-drug effectiveness and safety, we can expect little else from an industry that is self-regulating.

Other Prescription Diets

We have discussed in some detail two of the most blatant examples of the failure of medical diets for pets to provide the safety and efficacy we all expect of drugs. Feline bladder problems and diabetes are by no means the only diseases for which pet food companies have marketed their therapeutic diets. In fact, there are few medical conditions in pets for which there is not a special diet that claims to manage that condition. A full complement of these diets will rival the traditional drug pharmacy in the typical veterinary facility for numbers of products stocked! Diets exist for IBD (inflammatory bowel disease), skin allergies, obesity, senile dementia, kidney disease, and almost every other problem conceivable. What of these other products?

The key point to stress when considering any kind of diet for cats is the uniform inadequacy of all dry form commercial foods for this species. Whether or not a particular canned prescription-type diet is properly formulated for managing a particular medical condition in cats, it can be assumed with confidence that no dry kibbled food of this type is nutritionally sound for any cat. This point cannot be overemphasized. Cat owners must understand that breakfast cereal technology (called extrusion) used in the manufacture of all dry cat foods cannot, by its very nature, produce a food that is low in sugars and simple starches. Sugar and starch are toxic to cats in high quantities, which is anything over about 8 percent, on a dry matter basis. So, regardless of what else might be said for these types of diets, the dry form of these products should never be fed to any cat, healthy or diseased.

Beyond that, pet owners and veterinarians alike must harbor a healthy skepticism about these diets in general, no matter what form they take, because of their unjustified drug claims. Just as the FDA demands that human drugs, food products or devices for which claims of disease management or cure are made must be thoroughly and scientifically tested for safety and efficacy prior to use in patients, this same standard must be applied to pet foods used as drugs. Caveat emptor. Buyer beware! Your pet's health is at risk!

Fluoride in Pet Food—A Serious Health Risk for Both Dogs and Cats?

The Environmental Working Group (EWG) released a study of ten brands of manufactured dog foods analyzed for fluoride content. Eight had levels that could put dogs at risk for developing bone cancer, thyroid disease, and other health problems. For details, visit www.ewg.org/pethealthreport/fluoride-in-dog-food.

The EWG advises dog owners to avoid dog foods containing chicken by-product meal, poultry by-product meal, chicken meal, beef and bone meal, turkey meal, and lamb meal. These "meals" contain ground bone that is the source of fluoride that farmed animals accumulate. Ground bones from longer-living farm animals like dairy cattle, laying hens, and breeding stock are likely to contain higher levels of fluoride than shorter-living chickens, calves, and lambs. Fluorides accumulate in the body of farmed animals over time from such sources as phosphate fertilizers, phosphate supplements, bone meal and fish meal supplements, and pesticide and industrial-pollution-contaminated pastures and animal feed. The bones, fins, gills, and scales of fish are often high in fluoride, dioxins, and PCBs, being additional contaminants of concern in farmed salmon.

Cats may also be at risk from chronic fluoride poisoning when similar ingredients are included in their diets. The pet food industry should work with government regulators to establish fluoride safety-level limits in pet foods.

Thyroid disease, extremely common in cats, is also linked to fire-retardant bromide compounds in carpets, upholstery, and contaminated sea foods. Cats especially should be given pure water to drink, fluoridation being a health concern (for details visit www.drfoxvet.com).

Chapter 9

Finding Our Way Back:
A New Map for Feline Health

Today, the vast majority of the world's pet cats consume commercial cat foods, and most of these eat dry cat foods as an exclusive diet. First we must realize that there is absolutely no reason why we are feeding our cats commercially processed packaged foods today except for the fact that the pet food industry wants us to, and we have become accustomed to the perceived convenience of commercial pet foods. Thinking about a cat's natural diet automatically brings up the subject of raw meat as food for cats; after all, that is exactly what any free-living cat will consume regularly. Unfortunately, the subject of feeding raw meat to pets is mired in controversy created by pet food companies who fear erosion of their absolute control over the beliefs pet owners have about how to feed their pets. Billions of revenue dollars annually depend upon pet owners continuing to believe that only commercial pet foods can safely nourish their pets. Let's look at this controversial subject.

Is Feeding Raw Meat to Your Cat Safe?

Ask most veterinarians whether a raw meat diet is a good idea for any pet and you will almost certainly receive an unqualified No! as the answer. Most veterinarians believe that such practices will lead invariably to rampant food poisoning from bacterial contamination, as well as serious nutritional imbalances in pets fed homemade diets including raw meat. In reality, there is actually no scientific basis for this extreme bias against feeding the cat its evolutionary natural food, but it is a widespread misconception nonetheless.

Is Contamination a Concern?

If there can be no fundamental objection to the mere idea of raw meat as a diet for the cat, what legitimate objections might there be about the practical aspect of feeding raw meat to felines? The first objection would be the possibility of food poisoning from bacterial contamination of the meat. While this is certainly a possibility, just as food poisoning of humans who eat raw meat is always at least a possibility, the reality is highly controllable. Human-grade ground raw meats for pets are available today because of the growing popularity of the practice among pet owners. These meats are handled carefully by the processor, and frozen immediately after grinding.

All of the logical precautions against bacterial contamination that we observe in handling meat for our families apply to the practice of feeding meat to our cats. Further, cats will decline meat that is truly tainted. This is a survival trait with enormous value to the species. The same instincts that lead a cat to consume meat in the first place also tell it when not to eat a particular piece of meat in those instances where it senses danger in that meal.

What About Nutritional Adequacy of Raw Meat Diets?

The second criticism of raw meat diet for cats that authorities advance is the potential, even probable, nutritional inadequacy of such diets. We exploded that myth in Chapter 7.

Raw meat diets, properly designed, are proving considerably more nutritionally complete and balanced than their commercial, dry food rivals. Veterinarians and breeders who feed raw meat to pets find that they can correct virtually all of the problems caused by commercial dry foods with raw meat diets. Obesity, diabetes, urinary tract disease, and IBD simply do not occur in cats fed meat instead of commercial dry foods. It is important to note that we do not see nutritional deficiencies in properly balanced raw-meat-fed cats.

In the late 1940s through the 1950s, Dr. Francis Pottenger studied cats fed both raw meat and cooked meat diets. His discoveries were quite revealing at the time and highly relevant still today. Clearly we need additional long-term feeding studies of cat foods, to build upon our understanding of how important the cat's natural diet really is. As this debate grows, such studies on all forms of commercial and homemade diets, done properly by unbiased scientists, will be funded and get underway. Unfortunately, it will be years before we know the results with certainty, because such studies will have to be truly long-term to satisfy everyone. In the meantime, we have no reasonable alternative but to believe, from all of the evidence at hand, that properly designed raw meat diets are both safe and complete and balanced for health in all cats.

Is a raw meat diet the only way to properly nourish the pet cat? Although balanced raw meat diets are the gold standard for proper feline nutrition, there are canned commercial foods that appear to provide satisfactory results in many cats. Unfortunately, all commercially produced, cooked cat foods have the serious drawback of being highly over-processed, and as the Menu Foods pet food recall of 2007 showed, virtually all of these foods can become contaminated. Cats fed only commercial cooked foods as an exclusive diet run a significant risk of nutritional problems, even though canned foods are generally not as carbohydrate-toxic as dry cat foods. The solution for owners who prefer not to feed a balanced raw diet exclusively is to use balanced raw or lightly cooked meat together with occasional meals of good quality canned foods. A quality canned food is one with few, if any, cereal, vegetable or fruit ingredients.

Furthermore, we can certainly feed our cats food from our own tables, as long as our choices are high protein, low carbohydrate items such as cooked meats and even dairy products like yogurt and cheese. The pet food companies have long insisted that table scraps are poor foods for both dogs and cats. The irony in their message is that the ingredients in even good quality canned foods are nothing more than scraps from human food processing, cooked far more harshly than any food we might cook for ourselves, and stored in metal cans for weeks, months, or even longer. The mere fact that these scraps have vitamin and mineral supplements added to try to make up for the nutrients lost in this endless processing does not make commercial scraps any more desirable for our pets than the far fresher, and far more wholesome foods we serve to our own families. Pet nutrition is not complicated, even though the pet food industry desperately wants all of us to believe that it is.

The point, of course, is that we have taken a wrong road in our beliefs and practices about feeding our cats, and that mistake is costing our pets their very lives, and causing continued suffering. Fortunately, we can turn around and find our way back to a healthier lifestyle for our cats. Every day, new products become available to facilitate better nutrition for felines. Many owners even make the decision to grind their own meat and prepare their cat's balanced diet from scratch, a task that seems more daunting than it really is. Many are using portions of wholesome foods from their own diets to upgrade the commercial foods that they feed to their pets. This is a perfectly acceptable and logical thing to do.

However we decide to return to first principles in caring for our family felines, what is most important is that we shake off the cloak of misinformation provided by the pet food industry and begin to think for ourselves. We can do it; our cats are counting on us!

Some Useful Contacts

For cat food issues and transitioning on to raw food diet: www.feline-nutrition.org.

For dog food issues and transitioning on to a raw food diet: www.rawmeatybones.com.

For home-prepared dog and cat food recipes: www.dogcathomeprepareddiet.com.

For questions and answers about cat and doge health issues: www.DrFoxVet.com.

For veterinary formulated basic recipes and special diets for sick dogs and cats: www.secure.balanceit.com.

Chapter 10

Future Foods: Genetically Engineered or Go Organic?

You may not know it, but there is a war going on in the marketplace between advocates of organically certified foods for people and pets, and those who want to see genetically engineered foods filling all the shelves. The massive pet food recall in the spring of 2007 the largest in the industry's history not only raised many questions but also left many serious concerns unaddressed. One involves the use of genetically engineered (GE) ingredients in foods consumed by both animals and humans.

What Does Genetically Engineered Mean?

Genetically engineered (GE) or genetically modified (GM) plants sometimes dubbed Frankenfoods contain artificially inserted genes from viruses and other living organisms. This produces entirely novel chemicals that were never in our foods before, or in such quantities, and is done primarily to make crops resistant to herbicides and insect pests. Both our government and the multinational corporations selling these seeds of potential destruction to human, pet food and livestock feed manufacturers believe that Frankenfoods are safe, and that to believe otherwise is to not trust in science and progress.

On March 23, 2007, the New York State Department of Agriculture and Markets announced that they had found rat poison in contaminated wheat gluten imported from China. The poison is a chemical compound called aminopterin, but it was in such low concentrations that it was not thought to be the main cause of poisoning.

Aminopterin is used in genetic engineering biotechnology as a genetic marker. This use is included in U.S. Patent 6,130,207, filed November 5, 1997, (cell-specific molecule and method of importing DNA into a nucleus). This finding means that genetically engineered ingredients are in pet foods, but for the FDA to suggest there may be a connection, and health risks, could devastate an entire industry. That the testing labs used by the FDA in the 2007 pet food recall did not find any trace of aminopterin could be a cover-up, or due to poor handling of samples since light exposure quickly destroys this chemical.

Since pet foods show no labels to the contrary, and the FDA does not insist on the labeling of human foods when they contain GM ingredients, we have no way of knowing what we are really eating or feeding to our pets.

The U.S. government attempted to have genetically engineered seeds and foods included under the National Organic Standards when these standards were being formulated in the late 1990s, but was blocked by public outcry and a deluge of close to 300,000 letters of protest. Genetically engineered crops of corn, soy and canola that are herbicide resistant, and corn that produces its own insecticidal poison called Bt, get into the human food chain, and are put into livestock feed and pet foods with the government's blessing, and quite probably to the demise of the honey bee among other beneficial creatures, and a large agricultural sector of bee-pollination dependent orchard and field crops.

In 2006, an estimated 136 million acres of U.S. cropland was used to grow GM crops, and 89 percent of soybeans, 83 percent of cotton, and 61 percent of corn crops were genetically engineered.

Canola is also genetically engineered, and vegetable oils (cotton, canola and corn) along with soy protein and lecithin, are used widely in a variety of prepared foods for people and their pets.

In the 2007 Farm Bill, the government will be distributing some $33 billion in subsidies to help the nations' farmers over the next five years. But in actuality, around 65 percent of these tax dollars will go to 10 percent of the recipients. These are the big producers of the increasingly genetically engineered commodity crops that go into processed foods as soy protein, corn gluten and syrup, wheat flour and bran, rice flour, and oils of soy, corn and canola, with cotton byproducts being put into livestock feed, and more corn going in to the speculative and short-sighted bio-fuels market. Genetically engineered sugar beets will soon be planted widely as a source of sugar for the food industry. Beet pulp is a common ingredient in pet foods.

That a mere 2 percent of this agricultural spending will go to support vegetable and other whole food producers is indeed a lamentable misuse of public funds.

This Farm Bill funding is essentially for a highly subsidized, high-calorie and low nutrition program that makes convenience processed foods/meals and snacks relatively cheap in the marketplace and has helped spawn a nationwide epidemic of obesity and other health problems in both consumers/taxpayers and their pets.

Arguably the worst case scenario of nonsustainable industrial agriculture is this U.S. government commodity crop support program that subsidizes corn and soybean production—crops, now predominantly GM, that result in serious soil erosion and water pollution from agricultural pesticides and chemical fertilizers at an estimated $12.2 billion. Such subsidies are a disincentive to farmers to adopt more ecologically sound farming practices. The FDA has a wholly cavalier attitude toward feeding both livestock and pets the new GM varieties (some not yet approved for human consumption) of corn, soy, canola, rice, cotton (cottonseed cake and oil) and the other commodity crops and crop byproducts that are now dominating the agricultural landscape and world marketplace, regardless of documented adverse environmental consequences.

The FDA offers some restrictions where human consumption is involved, yet it refuses appropriate food labeling, including country of origin. The department claims, as its industry sponsors insist, that these crops and food products are substantially equivalent to conventionally bred varieties. This is totally incorrect. No scientifically valid, peer-reviewed food safety and quality studies were ever conducted or published before the biotechnology Life Science industry sought to monopolize world agriculture with patented varieties of GM seeds. Who can trust a government that continues to fast-track and approve new drugs that are only too often recalled soon after when people die or become gravely ill from adverse drug reactions, and continues to drag its heels on recalling and prohibiting harmful pesticides that are linked to infantile autism and Parkinson's disease?

What Are the Risks?

Numerous issues and unanswered questions surround the safety of GM foods.

The insecticidal poison Bt (Bacillus thuringiensis) is present in most genetically engineered U.S. commodity crops that go into animal feed and pet foods. High levels of Bt toxin in GM crops have made farmers ill and poisoned farm animals eating crop residues.

So-called overexpression can occur when spliced genes that manufacture chemicals such as Bt become hyperactive inside the plant and result in potentially toxic plant tissues. These are lethal not just to mealworms and other crop pests, but also to birds, butterflies, and other wildlife, and possibly to humans and their pets.

Researchers have also found that unlike conventionally bred crops, GM varieties are intrinsically unstable and prone to spontaneous mutations. When mutations occur, you can never know if what is being grown, harvested, processed, and consumed is really safe and nutritious.

The most disturbing review published in a highly credible, peer-reviewed journal confirms what concerned analysts and others have feared for several years. This is that GM seeds are genetically unstable because they are more prone than normal to undergo spontaneous mutations. This can mean that GM crops could produce novel, harmful proteins, excessive, even toxic amounts of normal nutrients, or become extremely deficient in same.

The inserted genes can have unforeseen consequences, so-called multiple pleiotropic effects. These unpredictable consequences of introducing a new genetic trait or quality include alterations in existing gene function and relationships with other genes. This could disrupt the regulation of metabolic pathways and the synthesis of proteins to keep cells and organs functioning normally. A dramatic example of this in animals is in the genetically engineered pigs that were created to carry human growth genes at the U.S. government's research facility in Beltsville, Maryland. These pigs became cripples, suffering from multiple health problems including arthritis and bone-growth deformities, and had impaired immune and reproductive systems.

Inserting alien genes into plants can be no less disruptive. The complex relationships between genes that make up the genome or genetic constitution of plants and all life forms mean that it is bad science to believe that it is safe to insert an artificially constructed (and patented) gene carrying a desired trait like herbicide or insect resistance. But this is precisely what the multinational corporations are doing without knowing or apparent concern for the consequences. Several recent studies have shown that the nutritional value and safety of GM crops and foods are to be questioned, and their consumption is to be avoided for health, environmental and ethical reasons (see Appendix B).

The herbicides glufosinate and glyphosate are liberally applied across the U.S. and in many other countries to millions of acres of crops genetically engineered to be resistant to these herbicides. These poisons are actually absorbed by the crops, while all else growing in the fields, and much of the surrounding aquatic life in rivers and lakes is wiped out. These widely used herbicides have caused kidney damage and other health problems in animals.

These herbicides and other agrichemicals, along with the insecticide Bt, are found in pet foods and the crops and crop byproducts fed to cattle, pigs, poultry, and dairy cows. Many nutritionists and health experts are linking the rise in human food allergies to the increased consumption of GM foods and food additives, especially genetically engineered soy products that contain novel proteins. The high incidence of skin allergies and other suspected allergies associated with digestive disorders and inflammatory bowel disease in dogs and cats may well be caused or aggravated by these novel proteins and other chemical contaminants in GM crop byproducts.

The British newspaper The Guardian reported on January 22, 2008, that Croplife International, the agricultural industry trade body of which the world's leading biotechnology companies, Monsanto, Syngenta, and BASF are members, resigned from a major international project to map out the future of agriculture in relation to climate change and world hunger. This was in response to the initial findings of some 4,000 scientists and experts from around the world that GM crops could pose problems for the developing world.

What You Can Do

Industrial agribusiness is indifferent toward the potential risks of GM crops and foods. Since pet foods show no labels to the contrary, and the FDA does not mandate the labeling of foods when they contain GM ingredients, we really have no way of knowing what we are eating or feeding our dogs and cats.

Make your opinions heard. Contact your state and federal elected representatives, food manufacturers and local grocery stores and tell them that you want to know what's in your food, and your pet's, and that you want labels on all GM foods and food products.

Look for the Certified Organic label when buying pet food, read the list of ingredients, or prepare organic foods from scratch. Until our governing bodies change their attitude, it's up to us to make sure we're protecting our health, and that of our dogs and cats, by becoming educated consumers.

Going Organic—the Best Alternative

Organic agriculture is the first medicine of holistic health and Earth-healing. Our reasoning behind the insistence on the inclusion of more and more Organically Certified foods on our market shelves and in pet foods has deep roots that we wish to share, because we see in organic farming practices the fundamental elements of good nutrition and health. The U.S. government now certifies food as organic when it has been produced without the use of synthetic chemical fertilizers and pesticides on crops, none of which can be genetically engineered, and without the use of antibiotics and growth-stimulating hormones and steroids in farmed animals that are generally raised more humanely in organic farming enterprises.

We human beings are surely at the time in our biological evolution when we must reflect upon the direction our lives and civilization have been taking and where we are going. We are at a crossroads, and we must choose which road to take, using common sense and compassion as guide and compass.

We are so cognitively disconnected from reality that we spray poisonous chemicals on the crops we feed to our children and rationalize such stupidity as the best and most efficient way to feed a hungry world and even to protect wildlife and biodiversity, and we are so emotionally disconnected from other animals that for economic reasons we justify incarcerating livestock in the cruel, intensive confinement systems of factory farming.

The Failed Promise of Industrial Agriculture's Science

The failure of the so-called Green Revolution that began in the 1970s ostensibly to end famine and hunger with the development of patented high-yield varieties of hybrid corn and other food crops that are now planted around the world was underscored in a report from the UK's Global Environmental Change Programme, funded by Britain's Economic and Research Council, and published in April 2000. Green Revolution crops, introduced in the late 1960s and early 1970s increased agricultural output and profits and provided much needed and affordable calories for the poor. But these crops failed to take up minerals such as iron and zinc from the soil.

The report states: High-yielding Green Revolution crops were introduced in poor countries to overcome famine. But these are now blamed for causing intellectual deficits, because they do not take up essential micronutrients. Iron deficiency disease contributes to increased infant mortality, and impaired brain development and learning ability, affecting an estimated 1.5 billion people in one-quarter of the earth's population, according to the author of this report, Dr. Christopher Williams.

It should also be added that such micronutrient deficiencies, also a nutritional problem in the West from deficient soils and crops, can impair the immune system, and related nutritional deficiencies and imbalances in various animal products, especially in the omega-3 and -6 polyunsaturated fatty acid ratios can impair brain development and cognitive functions.

Recent studies in Canada, the U.S., and the UK have shown that fruits and vegetables are less nutritious than thirty to fifty years ago, showing often marked deficiencies in iron, copper, zinc, calcium, sodium, phosphorus, protein, vitamin C and riboflavin, a disturbing finding attributable, in part, to the fast-growing and large-yielding varieties of crops being grown today for human consumption.

As for the use of chemical fertilizers, potassium fertilizer, for example, interferes with plants' magnesium uptake and phosphate absorption. Widely-used nitrogenous fertilizers can increase harmful nitrate levels in conventionally grown crops and lower the plant's vitamin C content, and although it can increase total protein content, the quality of the protein is inferior to organically grown crops, lacking in essential amino acids like lysine, which means lower quality food and inferior livestock feed.

None of these serious nutritional deficiency problems exist with organically grown foods. Studies comparing the nutrient content of organic versus conventionally grown crops report significantly lower levels of potentially toxic aluminum, mercury and lead in the organically grown, fewer nitrates, and higher levels of vitamin C and many essential trace minerals and other nutrients, notably boron, calcium, chromium, copper, iodine, iron, lithium, magnesium, manganese, molybdenum, phosphorus, potassium, selenium, silicon, sodium, sulfur, vanadium, and zinc.

Animal studies have shown that such functions as reproduction and resistance to infection may be adversely affected by conventionally produced foods as compared to organically produced ones.

We think we are wise to take our daily multivitamin and multimineral supplements, because they are insufficient in most of the foods we eat that do not come from certified organic farming systems, the produce from which have no such serious deficiencies.

But this taking of nutritional supplements or nutraceuticals, while sensible in moderation, is not real healing. It is yet another quick fix that the American Medical Association tried to monopolize and obliterate in 1995, and is seeking again to do so in concert with the pharmaceutical industry, by making all supplemental nutraceuticals prescription only, for the pharmaceutical industry.

Organic farming is the first medicine and ultimate antidote since, unlike conventional chemical-based agriculture, it does not deplete soils and crops and farmed animals, humans, and pets of essential nutrients.

The alliance of the pharmaceutical/petrochemical/medical/university/industrial complex is now beginning to break apart as study after study shows the health benefits and economic savings of humane and sustainable organic agriculture, and more and more human doctors as well as veterinarians are advocating the adoption of organically raised, whole (unrefined, unadulterated, and unprocessed) foods. Scientists are discovering that soils that are not farmed organically have less life and fewer nutrients for growing healthy and nutritious crops. Conventionally produced crops have serious nutrient deficiencies and imbalances because of the poor soil they came from, and from being grown on a synthetic chemical fertilizer diet of potash, phosphates, and nitrate of ammonia—junk food and speed for plants.

When governments, state and federal, and corporate America adopt the principles of bioethical responsibility, and we all begin to consume with conscience, we will experience such healing that we will probably no longer need dietary supplements or have to take potentially harmful drugs. We will have fewer cancers, heart attacks, osteoporosis, arthritis, depression, allergies, food poisonings, and fewer babies with birth defects and children with neurological, cognitive and emotional disorders. We will also have fewer obese cats and dogs who develop cancer, arthritis, chronic skin, liver, kidney, endocrine, immune system and a host of other diseases, many of which can be alleviated and prevented with better nutrition and purer foods.

We won't need to make animals suffer in laboratories to find cures for these diseases of Western civilization, or need genetically engineered pigs as organ donors, nor flocks of human-gene-bearing sheep and cattle herds providing us with new pharmaceuticals. Nor will we need to legitimize the creation of genetically engineered animals to manifest and suffer our genetic disorders and to serve as profitable models for developing new drugs to treat the myriad diseases we have brought upon ourselves, from cancer and chemosensitivity to immune-suppression and autoimmune diseases.

The replacement of animal-based foods with plant-based foods in the human diet could result in an 80 to 90 percent reduction in cancer, according to Colin Campbell, professor of nutritional biochemistry at Cornell University. A vegetarian diet is the best way for people to beat the obesity, diabetes, stroke, and heart attack epidemic that is sweeping across the consumptive West to other countries that adopt the Western diet and methods of industrial agriculture. Grass fed, organic, and free range animals and their produce, from beef and chicken to eggs and cheese, are more nutritious, and ethically more acceptable than the produce from animals incarcerated in cruel, and environmentally harmful factory feedlots and confinement sheds.

Several studies have shown that organic farming practices are good for wildlife, and help in the recovery of regional biodiversity. According to the UK's Institute of Science in Society, organic agriculture could save one-sixth of global energy use. Using that information, we can see that growing 10 percent of America's corn organically would save about 200 million gallons of oil. Organic agriculture could also reduce global greenhouse gas emissions by 30 percent if practiced more extensively. Organic farming also plays an important role in water purification and healthy soils that provide a natural filter and cleanser of rain water that is contaminated, often heavily, with a host of industrial chemical pollutants, and even pharmaceuticals and pesticides.

As for those who contend that organic agriculture cannot possibly feed the hungry world, University of Michigan professor Catherine Badgley and her colleagues have completed a three-year study of worldwide organic versus conventional farm yields and found that organic farming could produce three times as much as conventional farming practices in developing countries, and equal the productivity of conventional, petrochemical-based agriculture in the U.S. and other industrialized countries.

Responsible Choices

The most responsible choices we still have are to buy certified organic foods, and to avoid manufactured, convenience, and junk foods. The same holds true for what we buy for our pets and give them to eat.

THE HUMAN FOOD CHAIN IS COMPROMISED AS WELL

The business-as-usual liaison between the U.S. government and business interests is clearly exposed by The Boston Globe's article by reporter Diedtra Henderson at the height of American consumers' awakening to the hazards of imported foods virtually uninspected by our government. She revealed that federal authorities were working on a proposal to allow chickens raised, slaughtered, and cooked in China to be sold in the U.S.

Under current regulations, store labels do not have to indicate the meat's origin. In China, antibiotics and other drugs are used by poultry producers, and food safety and hygiene standards are dubious at best.

The poisoning and deaths of hundreds of people in Panama, as well as in Bangladesh, India, Haiti, Nigeria, and Argentina, from diethylene glycol, marketed from China as glycerine for inclusion in cough syrup, does not seem to be warning enough to our federal regulators. A late spring 2007 report said, as more U.S. acres are being dedicated to produce corn for ethanol production, U.S. dairy farmers who cannot get enough certified organic soybean and corn from U.S. producers were outsourcing to countries like China.

The explosion of imports was well documented by reporter Robert Cohen in the June 10, 2007, The Star-Ledger, who wrote that the FDA said it will inspect only 0.7 percent of the estimated 16.3 million shipments coming into the U.S. this year from 230 countries. The FDA blocked 77,260 of 14.9 million shipments in 2006 for health and safety reasons, up from 54,577 in 2005, but is only able to check up on a very small number of the 300,000 manufacturers that make FDA-regulated products like pharmaceuticals and food ingredients shipped to the U.S. Without foreign government collaboration, experts say, the United States will never have enough inspectors given the volume of imports.

Many pet owners are willing to cook healthful meals for their dogs and cats, or find a supplier whom they can really trust, yet ruefully admit that they rarely if ever cook for themselves. They eat out or zap prepared foods made by dog knows whom in the microwave oven, the use of which is actually considered unsafe in some other countries.

Support local farmers' markets, organic producers, food co-ops, and whole food suppliers. We will then begin to break free from our addiction to convenience and prepared foods, the cheapness of which is an illusion because billions of our tax dollars go to subsidize the production of the major crops used by the big agribusiness commodity producers, livestock industry, and manufactured food wholesalers. And we pay again with the health problems we and our pets develop on these kinds of food and diets that are highly advertised on TV and elsewhere, and are even included in school lunch programs and hospital food services to patients across the U.S.

All hospitals, as well as schools and other institutions, should follow Kaiser Permanente's recent initiative to provide organic, whole foods to patients in all their hospitals.

Most people a generation ago prepared their own meals from scratch and knew the source of every ingredient they fed to their loved ones, including their pets. Cooking was a necessity we eat to live. Good cooking comes not simply from the love of cooking but from cooking with love. This love includes concern for how the food items were produced, for their nutritional value, quality, and especially humaneness when it comes to produce from farmed animals.

The act of cooking for ourselves and loved ones, including our pets, should not become a lost art, or abandoned because we have no time. The act of cooking with love is tantamount to an act of civil disobedience. If the manufacturers of prepared, convenience foods had their way, it would be outlawed. So kitchen anarchists and culinary comrades unite! And try the pet food recipes suggested in Appendix A.

Chapter 11

Diet, Nutrition, Health and Behavior: Surveys and Overview

Between March 2004 and March 2005, readers of coauthor Michael Fox's nationally syndicated "Animal Doctor" newspaper column wrote to him about the hundreds of different health and behavior problems afflicting their cats and dogs. These were reviewed and tabulated. Many of the problems had received veterinary attention but had not been cured. Here is an overview of the ten most common health and behavior problems from these letters.

Health problems in dogs:
- skin problems itching, hair loss, hot spots/raw areas and acral-lick granulomas (sores that never heal)
- adverse reactions to vaccinations and anti-flea and tick medications
- lameness/arthritis
- seizures and congestive heart failure tied for fourth place
- various cancers

Behavioral problems in dogs:
- coprophagia and pica (eating stools, dirt, grass)
- aggression toward other dogs and toward people
- fear/phobias, especially to fireworks and sudden noises
- obsessive compulsive disorders like tail-chasing and carpet-digging
- urinating in the house, separation anxiety, excessive barking, and incontinence in female dogs all tied in fifth place

The top five health problems in cats:

- skin problems: itching, hair pulling, raw spots, and hair loss
- feline urologic syndrome (urinary bladder inflammation and calculi/blockage of urine)
- chronic diarrhea, possibly inflammatory bowel disease
- kidney failure and adverse reactions to vaccinations and anti-flea meds tied for fourth place
- repeated vomiting of food

The top behavioral problem in cats:

- house soiling, most often with urine (and not associated with FUS), but frequently with feces as well
- aggression toward humans (in some cases possibly linked to hyperthyroidism)
- aggression toward other cats in the home
- biting too hard during play and love biting while being petted
- addiction to dry food, senile dementia, and spraying by mainly neutered males shared fifth place

More Revealing Pet Health Surveys

The American Veterinary Medical Association published the following facts and figures on the most prevalent health problems in cats and dogs in the U.S. causing owners to seek veterinary treatment, compiled by the Veterinary Pet Insurance Company of Brea, California.

For the second year in a row, urinary tract infections topped the list for cats as the most common medical condition. Veterinary visits for skin allergies resulted in the most claims for dogs in 2005, bypassing ear infections, which topped the list in 2004.

Claims by incident in 2005 for dogs:

1. Skin allergies
2. Ear infections

3. Stomach upsets
4. Bladder infections
5. Benign tumors
6. Osteoarthritis
7. Sprains
8. Eye infections
9. Enteritis
10. Hypothyroidism

Claims by incidence for cats in 2005:

1. Urinary tract infections
2. Stomach upsets
3. Kidney disease
4. Skin allergies
5. Respiratory infections
6. Diabetes
7. Ear infections
8. Colitis
9. Eye infections
10. Wound infections

A 2004 listing in order of frequency of the ten most common claims of over 6,400 medical conditions that Veterinary Pet Insurance Inc. received from cat and dog owners certainly reveals a high incidence of the most probable junk food related diseases in the dog and cat population of the U.S., with the exception of bite abscesses in cats and soft tissue trauma in dogs, both conditions being associated with animals who are allowed to free-roam.

For dogs:

1. Ear infection
2. Stomach inflammation
3. Skin irritation
4. Tumors/growths
5. Skin infection/hot spots

6. Urinary tract infection

7. Osteoarthritis

8. Hypothyroidism

9. Inflammation of the intestinal tract

10. Soft tissue trauma

For cats:

1. Urinary tract infection

2. Stomach inflammation

3. Kidney disease

4. Abscess

5. Diabetes

6. Hyperthyroidism

7. Inflamed colon

8. Conjunctivitis

9. Ear infection

10. Skin irritation

Aside from the few health problems in dogs, and especially cats, from being allowed outdoors to roam free (eating garbage, getting into fights, and contacting sick animals), all of the above medical conditions are worth careful scrutiny. These are occurring in animals who are essentially confined indoors most of their lives. So what is brought into their environments from the outside to cause so many health problems?

Topping the list are the kinds and quality of food, water, routine preventive medicines (especially vaccinations and anti-flea and parasite drugs), house and garden chemicals, and, last but not least, emotional stress in the animal's life, notably separation anxiety, boredom, and social conflict, especially in group-housed cats. In-home chemical contaminants play some role in certain diseases, like the association between hyperthyroidism in cats and bisphenols lining cat food cans and water bottles, and fire-retardant bromide compounds (in the carpets, furniture upholstery, curtains, and owners' clothes) that turn into toxic dust.

Pets Don't Have to Suffer These Problems

Most of these dog and cat health and behavioral problems are preventable, and in many instances are effectively treated by veterinarians who use a holistic medical approach. This includes behavioral counseling, coupled with preventive health-care education for cat and dog owners, and especially for those who have recently purchased (but ideally adopted) a new kitten or puppy.

Most of these health and behavioral problems, causing much animal suffering and emotional and financial cost to the owners, should and can become something of the past when the basic principles of holistic veterinary preventive medicine and responsible animal care are put into practice, genetic susceptibilities of certain breeds of dogs and cats and individual genetic abnormalities notwithstanding. The cure is for pet owners to provide the right nutrition/diet, and establish a bond with the animal based as much on understanding as on affection. This bond is based on having some knowledge of the animal's behavior and emotional, social, environmental and physical needs, and includes providing the best possible environment for the animal. In the U.K., under the recently amended animal protection act, this is considered a duty of all pet owners.

Pure Breed Genetic Concerns

Another duty is correct breeding one of the cardinal principles of animal rights and welfare, and holistic veterinary medicine. A major ethical and animal welfare issue is the commercial propagation, purchase and ownership of purebred dogs and cats prone to diseases of hereditary origin. This happens all too often unethical owners breed animals for particular traits and qualities, without paying attention to bloodlines. These backyard breeders (as opposed to responsible and knowledgeable breeders) breed dogs too closely and end up perpetuating hereditary diseases and conditions, as documented by the American Association of Veterinarians for Animal Rights.

The rising popularity of pure-breed varieties of cats will mean a market-driven surge in genetic abnormalities and inheritable diseases in the domestic feline population similar to what we see in the canine population which was in part brought on, critics contend, by the erroneous public belief that AKC registration of a puppy-mill bred pup was like a Good Housekeeping seal of approval. But no guarantees of genetic soundness could be given because these profit-driven backyard breeders did not keep any progeny testing records, i.e. finding out if the pups they were selling were genetically sound or not. Responsible breeders keep and closely follow such records.

Pet Food Industry Capitalizing on Pure Breed Trend

The pet food industry is now capitalizing on the genetic/ nutrition-linked diseases of dogs and cats by developing a new generation of designer and prescription diets specifically formulated to treat various heritable diseases. This so-called nutritional genomics research to develop and market special diets for genetically impaired pets does nothing to prevent the occurrence and reduce the incidence of genetic/nutrition related diseases. So breeders need to do a better job, and buyers of purebred cats and dogs must beware and must look closely at breeders' credentials. Reputable and responsible breeders welcome this scrutiny, and are always happy to show the pedigrees (family trees) of their animals.

Better Nutrition, Fewer Health and Behavior Problems

Below is a short summary of some the most common health and behavioral problems in dogs and cats that we know are associated with manufactured pet foods because they are ameliorated and often eliminated after the afflicted animals are fed the kind of organically certified, biologically appropriate and health-maximizing whole food diets that we advocate, ones that are neither highly processed nor full of synthetic additives/supplements.

Cats

Constant shedding; frequent fur-ball vomiting; obsessive grooming to the point of self-mutilation; hyperactivity, increased irritability/aggression; house soiling/litter box avoidance; vomiting frequently after meals; food addiction (usually to dry foods); constant food soliciting/hunger; pica (ingesting all manner of non-food materials); chronic constipation; megacolon; irritable bowel syndrome; obesity; depression; diabetes; blindness; liver and kidney disease; halitosis and chronic dental disease; impaired healing and immunity.

Dogs

Constant shedding; noxious body/skin odor; excessive scratching and chewing to the point of self-mutilation; acral-lick granulomas; frequent vomiting of food; acid reflux; constant flatulence; acute bloat; coprophagia; pica; excessive drinking/polydipsia; constant food soliciting/hunger; increased aggression/irritability/hyperactivity; depression/hypoactivity; chronic ear and anal gland problems; acute pancreatitis; liver and kidney diseases; depression; aggression; epileptic seizures; halitosis and chronic dental disease; impaired healing and immunity.

Proper Care Is Another Right

The other right of all domestic animals, a duty of all pet owners when their animals are sick, is to appropriate veterinary care. Such care must begin with a more conservative approach to prescribing and administering potentially harmful and often unnecessary vaccinations and medications, especially those used to control fleas and ticks, that are wrongly touted under the banner of preventive medicine.

Still too many veterinarians do not consider changing their sick patients' diets. Instead they practice iatrogenic (harmful consequence) medicine, first by endorsing the continued feeding of potentially harmful diets, then by prescribing potentially harmful drugs.

Antibiotics and anti-fungal drugs are widely prescribed, especially for chronic skin, ear, and dental diseases, along with long-term treatment with prednisone/corticosteroids for a variety of all-too-common skin problems and inflammatory bowel disorders in dogs and cats, all of which can often be cured by a simple change in diet to a whole food, organically certified, additive- and synthetic-supplement-free diet.

Animals with arthritis/degenerative joint disease can similarly benefit from improved nutrition and especially from omega-3

TOO MANY VACCINES CAUSE PROBLEMS

Adverse vaccination reactions resulting in disease (so-called vaccinosis) include injection-site fibrosarcomas in cats, and various immune-system dysfunction diseases, possibly hyperthyroidism, inflammatory bowel disease, various chronic skin conditions, and kidney disease. More research has been done in dogs, where certain breeds and lines are particularly prone to develop vaccinosis. Conditions include encephalitis, seizures, polyneuropathy (weakness, incoordination and muscle atrophy), hypertrophic osteodystrophy (shifting lameness and painful joints), autoimmune thyroiditis and hypothyroidism, liver, kidney and bone marrow failure variously associated with autoimmune hemolytic anemia, immune mediated thrombocytopenia. The increased recognition of vaccinosis means a more conservative approach to vaccinating dogs, cats, ferrets, and other companion animals. (See Appendix D for more details.)

fatty acid supplement with chondroitin, glucosamine, and MSM rather than being put on long-acting prednisone. Steroid drugs have many harmful consequences, including increased susceptibility to infection, diabetes, muscular weakness and osteoporosis, Cushing's disease, increased appetite, agitation, and aggression.

The wholesale prescribing of glucocorticosteroids to arthritic dogs and cats is another component of profitable iatrogenic veterinary practice that would not be needed if dogs and cats were not fed diets deficient in various essential fatty acids and other micronutrients needed to maintain normal joint structure and function. Such medication disrupts animals' immune and endocrine systems, already severely challenged (as are our own) by thousands of environmental toxins. This kind of treatment creates more health problems, more cases of cystitis in dogs and sinusitis in cats, for example, because dogs are more susceptible to bacterial infections of the urinary bladder when put on long-term corticosteroid medication, as cats are to nasal sinus and upper respiratory tract infection.

Arthritic dogs and cats are put on safer non-steroidal anti-inflammatory drugs NSAIDS and just as in humans (resulting in recent multi-billion dollar NSAID market recalls), this can have harmful, even fatal consequences. Animals (and humans) already at risk from cardiovascular, liver, and kidney diseases have this risk revealed when NSAIDS cause kidney or liver failure, heart disease, and circulatory problems. These iatrogenic diseases, confounded by genetic variability and susceptibility, are the legacy of our petrochemical/pharmaceutical age and way of thinking, now further confounded by molecular science, genetic determinism, and the genetically engineered products of the agricultural biotechnology food and drug industries.

Dogs are especially susceptible to developing neurological and behavioral problems ranging from seizures, often diagnosed as idiopathic epilepsy, and obsessive-compulsive disorders, and are put on barbiturates and various psychotropic drugs, often for the rest of their lives, the long-term consequences of which can be detrimental to the animal's quality of life. In many instances a change to a whole food diet, additive free, and in some cases containing no wheat products, can help either prevent or reduce the severity and frequency of seizures, and help alleviate various neuro-behavioral disorders.

The final profitable top-off to such veterinary iatrogenics is to sell the client expensive prescription-only special diets, ones now often tailored to help ameliorate genetically linked diseases in pure breeds. These special diets are usually from the same big label companies whose products helped make the animals sick in the first place, that most animals do not like to eat, and that may contain some of the same ingredients that made the animal sick in the first place.

This kind of veterinary practice has become the norm, and we find it especially in what we call the shopping mall McVeterinary Hospital. Many are part of nation-wide franchised chains. They sell junk pet foods and treats and prescription diets. They promote over-vaccination and around-the-year treatment with potentially harmful anti-parasitic drugs to protect rarely exposed, low-risk animals from viral infections and parasitic infestations, preying on clients' fears and sense of duty, responsibility, and guilt for noncompliance.

They also offer routine, i.e. normative, surgical procedures such as declawing cats (the amputation of the final joint of a cat's toes) and ear cropping dogs to their trusting clients, procedures that outside the U.S. are considered unethical and often even illegal.

New Thinking Is Needed for Our Pets' Feeding

Not all adverse food reactions are the fault of the pet food manufacturer because no single pet food is ideal for all animals, even though the industry still makes this false claim. A specific supplement or whole food ingredient could be harmful to certain genotypes/breeds, and biochemical individuality means that nutritional needs are not identical for all members of the same species. It is no coincidence that one of the biggest American pet food manufacturers in the U.S. is now selling pet health insurance policies.

Significant advances in nutritional genomics that can help identify which particular breeds and individuals should not be fed certain types of pet food will only come with complete and accurate labeling of manufactured pet foods, and impeccable record keeping by manufacturers and attending veterinarians.

Some breeds are, for example, at risk from certain trace minerals like copper and zinc, or amino acid deficiencies like taurine, or are allergic to certain ingredients like wheat that can cause seizures, and in Irish setters, an inflammatory bowel disease.

Likewise, advances in nutritional epigenetics, where certain food ingredients, or lack thereof, can influence gene function and expression, may well reveal harmful developmental consequences to the offspring of dogs and cats fed commercial pet foods. As shown by researchers at the Royal Veterinary College, London, rat offspring of mothers fed junk food during pregnancy and lactation tend to overeat, chose junk food over healthier alternatives, and have increased susceptibility to obesity and type II diabetes.

As a more informed consumer populace says no to junk/fast/convenience foods (for themselves and their pets), so the days are numbered for the other agribusiness food and beverage industry subsidiary, namely the mainstream commercial pet food manufacturer, unless it chooses to meet the rising public demand for safe and nutritious food for all. And that, surely, would be an ethically enlightened business decision, since continued resistance to change, denial, lack of accountability, and defense of the status quo are ultimately counterproductive and self-defeating regardless of the $15 billion annual income enjoyed by U.S. pet food manufacturers.

But public trust will be hard to regain after the debacle of the largest pet food recall ever in the U.S. in the spring of 2007 of some 60 million containers bearing scores of different manufacturer and supplier labels, including all the big brand names, that left an estimated 8,500 dogs and cats dead, and harmed hundreds of thousands of others.

There is a new generation of commercial cat and dog foods, from raw to freeze-dried, canned to dry, that contain organically certified, whole food ingredients properly formulated and balanced, (i.e. not loaded with cereal and meat industry byproducts), that are now appearing on grocery shelves, and being marketed by local and national supply networks. Also several good books are available for preparing homemade cat and dog food. This trend goes hand in hand with increasing consumer demand for organically produced, minimally processed foods as more health and environmentally conscious shoppers vote with their dollars and sense, and with veterinarians recognizing the harmful consequences of most manufactured pet foods and treating their animal patients accordingly.

The words of health and fitness guru ninety-three year old Jack LaLanne are as relevant to what we eat ourselves as to what people feed to their cats and dogs. He asserts, quite simply, If man makes it, don't eat it.

PET FOOD RECALLS AND SAFETY ISSUES

The Partnership for Food Protection and the Food and Drug Administration announced August 1, 2011, the launch of the Pet Event Tracking Network (PETNet), which is a secure, web-based information exchange system that will allow the FDA and federal and state agencies to share initial information about pet-food related incidents, such as illness associated with the consumption of pet food or pet food product defects. PETNet's voluntary information exchange, surveillance, and alert system is designed to provide a real-time mechanism for sharing information about emerging pet food related illnesses and product defects among the FDA, other federal agencies and the states, the FDA's Center for Veterinary Medicine (CVM) said in a CVM Update. The system is accessible to PETNet members, who are federal, state, and territorial government officials responsible for the regulation of pet food products and the investigation of disease outbreaks in companion animals. The concept for PETNet was developed in response to the 2007 melamine pet food recall. Pet owners can get news about recalls from Susan Thixton at www.truthaboutpetfood.com, Dr. Karen Becker at healthypets.mercola.com, and Dr. Michael W. Fox at www.drfoxvet.com.

Cooking For Your Pet:
Dog and Cat Food Recipes

The following basic recipes will provide a good start and a sound foundation for you to prepare balanced diets for your dog or cat. You can vary the kind of ingredients you select and that your animal enjoys, provided you stick to the basic balanced quantities in the recipes. Whenever possible, use organically certified ingredients because of higher safety standards (no pesticides used), and superior nutritional value than conventional produce.

Chickens, for example, fed on certified organic feed have more vitamin E, beta carotene and omega-3 fatty acids, while organically grown vegetables contain as much as 40 percent more antioxidants including flavonoids, higher levels of beneficial iron and zinc, and lower levels of harmful nitrate, lead, mercury, and aluminum.

Familiarize yourself with beneficial herbal, vitamin, mineral, amino-acid, and other food supplements, and have your veterinarian consider adding various such nutraceuticals to your pet's diet when there are specific health problems that can be helped, with these supplements such as kidney, liver, and heart disease, skin and joint problems, allergies, etc.

Dr. Michael Fox's Homemade Natural
Dog Food Recipe

6 pounds of chicken or turkey drumsticks or 4 pounds of chicken or turkey thighs, skin removed (to produce about 3 pounds meat)

1 pound chicken or turkey hearts*

½ pound chicken or turkey liver*

    2 cups uncooked brown rice or barley

    1 cup rolled oats or whole wheat or rice pasta

    1 cup grated sweet potato, yam, or carrot*

    8 cups water

    1 tablespoon cider vinegar

    2 tablespoons unflavored gelatin

    4 eggs, yolk plus whites

    ½ cup cottage cheese or live yogurt*

    4 tablespoons flax seed oil*

    1 teaspoon nutritional yeast or 200 mg. vitamin B complex*

    4 tablespoons bone meal (sterilized for human consumption, not garden fertilizer) or 4 tablespoons of crushed tablets of calcium lactate, citrate, or carbonate supplement with magnesium, boron.

Combine all the above ingredients except those marked with an asterisk.

Add water, bring to boil then simmer for 15 to 20 minutes and stir. Add more water as needed until lightly cooked and tender.

Add raw vegetables, livers, and hearts to the hot mixture and stir. If runny, thicken with a little oat bran.

When contents are cool, debone legs. Discard bones in a safe container (Dogs should not be given cooked bones to eat since they can splinter and cause internal damage.) but save the end-cartilage of the joints and bone ends and chop this cartilage up very small.

Chop up the meat, liver, and hearts into dime-sized cubes. Add back in with diced cartilage.

Chill this meat-vegetable mix in the refrigerator for 30 minutes then add ingredients marked with an asterisk.

Portion out cup-sized measurements and place in muffin tins or plastic storage bags and freeze.

Thaw out as needed. Serve one cupful of this recipe for a 30-pound dog twice daily. Serve thawed at body temperature or frozen to gnaw on outdoors in hot weather.

This recipe may be simply put into a food processor (minus the water) and fed raw, provided the dog is transitioned to accept raw food and maintains optimal weight.

To transition your dog on to this new food, mix increasing amounts of your dog new food with decreasing amounts of the old food over a seven-day period. This enables adaptation and avoids possible digestive upset. It is advisable to monitor the animal's body condition so as to avoid either overfeeding orderfeeding.

Different animals have slightly different nutritional needs according to age, temperament, amount of physical activity and health status. Large dogs require less food per pound body weight, so adjust according to appetite and weight gain, and especially if deep-chested and prone to bloat, give three to four smaller meals per day.

For dogs under 30 pounds and for overweight and less active dogs, use one cup of uncooked rice in the recipe. For large dogs over 70 pounds adjust amount served to about one cup per 30 pounds of body weight.

Things to Remember

- Some dogs are allergic to dairy products, eggs, and wheat, so adjust diet accordingly.
- Grass-fed beef or lamb/mutton, heart, and liver can be used as alternative animal protein sources in the same quantities as above for poultry.
- A teaspoon of finely chopped dandelion leaves, wheat grass, or parsley and four to six drops of cod liver oil or salmon oil, or a teaspoon of unsalted organic butter mixed into one meal two or three times a week (per 30 to 40 pounds body weight) may be beneficial. Gradually working up to 1 teaspoon of turmeric per day in the food (for a 30- to 40-pound dog) may help give old dogs more zest and ease arthritic joint pain.
- Avoid giving onion, chocolate, macadamia nuts, raisins, grapes, and for some dogs, garlic.
- Because foods vary considerably in their nutrient content it is advisable to give the dog a human one-a-day

multivitamin and multi-mineral supplement crushed in the food, calculating one half the human daily recommended amount for a 50-pound dog. Pfizer's Pet Tabs are an acceptable daily doggy supplement and Platinum Canine Performance health supplements for dogs, available only through veterinarians, offer considerable nutraceutical benefits.

Keep teeth clean by getting dogs, especially toy breeds, used to a daily brushing. The best and safest natural tooth-cleaner is a raw, scalded (to kill off bacteria), 3-inch to 4-inch piece of beef shank, soup, or marrow bone.

Dr. Michael Fox's Homemade Natural Cat Food Recipe

6 pounds of chicken or turkey drumsticks or 4 pounds of chicken or turkey thighs, skin removed (to produce about 3 pounds of meat)

1 pound chicken or turkey hearts* (or substitute 4 gm. (4,000mg.) taurine*)

½ pound chicken or turkey liver* (or substitute 40,000 IU vitamin A and 1600 IU vitamin D)

2 cups water

1 tablespoon cider vinegar

2 tablespoons unflavored gelatin

4 eggs, yolk plus whites

¼ pound unsalted butter

½ cup cottage cheese, or "live" yogurt*

4 gm (4,000mg.) salmon oil*

1 teaspoon nutritional yeast or 200 mg. vitamin B complex*

800 mg. vitamin E*

4 tablespoons bone meal (sterilized for human consumption, *not* garden fertilizer), or 4 tablespoons of crushed

tablets of calcium lactate, citrate, or carbonate supplement with magnesium, boron. If vitamin D is included in this, give less vitamin. D supplement above when using the vitamin A and D substitute for liver.

Combine all the above ingredients except those marked with an asterisk.

Add water, bring to boil then simmer for 15 minutes.

Stir, and add more water as needed until lightly cooked and tender.

Add raw livers and hearts to the hot mixture and stir.

When contents are cool, debone legs. Discard bones in a safe container (Cats should not be given cooked bones to eat since they can splinter and cause internal damage.) but save the end-cartilage of the joints and bone ends and chop this cartilage up very small.

Chop up the meat, liver, and hearts into dime-sized cubes. Add back in with diced cartilage.

Chill this meat-vegetable mix in the refrigerator for 30 minutes then add ingredients marked with an asterisk.

Portion out cup-sized measurements and place in muffin tins or plastic storage bags and freeze.

Thaw out as needed. Serve at body temperature.

As with the dog food recipe, this recipe may be simply put into a food processor (minus the water) and fed raw, provided the cat is transitioned to accept raw food and maintains optimal weight.

Monitor the animal's body condition so as to avoid either overfeeding or underfeeding. Base this on the average cat consuming one-third of a capful three or four times a day.

Growing animals need to be fed smaller portions six to eight times per day. If the animal has a preexisting medical condition, consult with your veterinarian before changing the diet.

To one of these meals each day add three to four drops of salmon or cod liver oil, and a sprinkling of taurine.

A daily multivitamin and multimineral supplement is also advisable. One that also supplies essential amino-acids and is recommended by feline vets is called Platinum Performance Feline Wellness.

Once every two weeks add finely chopped wheat grass, alfalfa or parsley.

Things to Remember

- Different animals have slightly different nutritional needs according to age, temperament, amount of physical activity and health status).
- Ideally all ingredients should be organically certified.
- Some cats are allergic to dairy products and eggs, so adjust diet accordingly.
- Grass-fed beef, heart, and liver can be used as alternative animal protein sources in the same quantities as
- Transition your cat gradually onto this new diet by mixing increasing amounts of your cat's new food with decreasing amounts of the old food over a seven-day period to avoid possible digestive upset.

Keep teeth clean by giving your cat a scalded (to kill bacteria) raw chicken wing tip with skin on it to chew every three to four days or thin strips of scalded raw beef heart or shank meat—the tougher the better! Avoid addictive and potentially harmful dry foods that do little to keep teeth clean.

If you wish to "go raw" and prepare your own cat food, you may instead wish to follow the recipes advocated by Anne Jablonski (catnutrition.org) that veterinarian Dr. Lisa Pierson supports, which are adapted from the trailblazing work by Feline Future (felinefuture.com).

Dr. Pierson (catinfo.org) also gives some the names of suppliers of frozen and canned cat foods that meet the science-based and medical criteria of acceptance-based on the detailed review of feline nutrition by Dr. Debra L. Zoran. These include grain-free Evo, Nature's Variety, Wellness, and Wysong's Archetype.

Dr. Fox's Cat and Dog Treats

Make your own pet treats unless you buy ideally certified organic treats free of additives, preservatives, and coloring agents, made locally or in the U.S. and certainly not imported. One or two treats should only be given three or four times a day to avoid addiction, pets becoming overweight, or pets refusing to eat their regular food.

Cat Treat Recipe

1 cup of rice flour or buckwheat (avoid wheat and high gluten cereals)
¾ cup of sardines or mackerel in oil; or two eggs,
½ cup chopped liver (chicken or beef)
1 tablespoon of grated white cheese or ¾ cup of fatty ground beef, chicken, turkey, or lamb
1 tablespoon of cod liver oil

Mix all ingredients well, adding sufficient water to make a soft dough.

Roll out into very thin strips and bake in a preheated oven at 315 degrees for 20 to 25 minutes. Switch off oven and let cool in oven to crispen but not burn.

Break into small dime-sized pieces and store in an airtight container in the refrigerator.

Dog Treat Recipe

2 cups of buckwheat, rice, or rye flour (avoid wheat and high gluten cereals)) as a binder for either
½ cup of ground chicken, turkey, lamb, beef liver, or ground beef, and one egg or two eggs and two tablespoons of peanut butter or grated white cheese
1 tablespoon cod liver, flax, or olive oil

Mix all ingredients well, adding sufficient water to make a soft dough.

Roll out into very thin strips and bake in a preheated oven at 315 degrees for 20 to 25 minutes. Switch off oven and let cool in oven to crispen but not burn.

Break into small nickel-sized pieces and store in an airtight container in the refrigerator.

 For variation, add mashed, cooked yam or sweet potato instead of grated cheese or peanut butter. Try spicing cat and dog treats with ½ teaspoon of ground cinnamon or ginger, even cat nip for cats and Brewer's (not baking) yeast for both.

 Crush three human daily multivitamin and mineral supplements into each batch for good measure.

MW Fox Dog Food

10 kg dog Kcal/D		%DM	g/1000 Kcal		g/d		% As Fed	g/100 Kcal	g/d
Kcal/kg	345	430	345	430	345	430		102.2	
Protein	22	35	6.38	8.14	42.5	54.2	9.9	9.7	64.51
Carbohydrate	57	27	16.52	6.28	110.0	41.8	13.3	13.0	86.65
Dietary Fiber	4	4	1.16	0.93	7.7	6.2	0.2	0.2	1.30
Ash	9	9	2.61	2.09	17.4	13.9	1.6	1.6	10.43
Total Fat	8	25	2.32	5.81	15.4	38.7	2.5	2.4	16.29
Moisture							72.5		
Calcium	1	1.25	0.29	0.29	1.9	1.9	0.4	0.34	2.28
Phosphorus	0.8	1.00	0.23	0.23	1.5	1.5	0.5	0.15	0.98
Magnesium	0.09	0.11	0.03	0.03	0.2	0.2	0.0	0.03	0.20
Potassium	0.6	0.75	0.17	0.17	1.2	1.2	0.1	0.12	0.78
Sodium	0.3	0.37	0.09	0.09	0.6	0.6	0.1	0.1	0.78
Chlorine	0.45	0.56	0.13	0.13	0.9	0.9	1.4	1.42	9.45
	mg/kg		mg/100 Kcal		mg/d		mg/kg	mg/100 Kcal	mg/d
Iron	80	99.74	2.3	2.3	15.4	15.4	14.0	1.37	9.12
Zinc	120	149.61	3.5	3.5	23.2	23.2	11.0	1.08	7.17
Copper	7.3	9.10	0.2	0.2	1.4	1.4	1.0	0.10	0.65
Manganese	5	6.23	0.1	0.1	1.0	1.0	4.0	0.39	2.61

Cats Nutritional Requirements

Lean mature cat	Bw Kg	KcalME/d
	6	332

Nutrient	Range of adequate nutrient intakes for cats based on a min. and max. fat intake						MWFox Cat Food* (89.2 Kcal/100g at 76.5% Moisture) Actual Analysis		
	% DM		g/100 Kcal		5 kg cat g/d		% DM	g/100 Kcal	6 kg cat g/d
	Max Fat	Min Fat	Max Fat	Min Fat	Max Fat	Min Fat			
Kcal ME/100g	500	365					380.0		
Protein	52	79	10.4	21.6	34.5	71.7	73.0	19.17	63.7
Fat	37.5	10.5	7.5	2.9	24.9	9.5	12.9	3.36	11.2
Ash	10	10	2.0	2.7	6.6	9.1	9.7	2.58	8.6
Fiber	0.5	0.5	0.1	0.1	0.3	0.5	0.2	0.05	0.2
	% DM		g/100 Kcal		g/d		% DM	g/100 Kcal	g/d
Calcium	1.4	1	0.28	0.27	0.93	0.91	1.6	0.43	1.4
Phosphorus	1.1	0.8	0.22	0.22	0.73	0.73	0.9	0.25	0.8
Magnesium	0.11	0.08	0.02	0.02	0.07	0.07	0.1	0.08	0.3
Sodium	0.29	0.2	0.06	0.06	0.19	0.18	1.2	0.33	1.1
Potassium	0.86	0.6	0.17	0.16	0.57	0.54	0.6	0.17	0.6
Chlorine	.43	0.3	0.086	0.08	0.29	0.27	1.4	0.37	1.2
Sulphur							0.8	0.21	0.7
	mg/kg		mg/100 Kcal		mg/d		mg/kg	mg/100 Kcal	mg/d
Iron	114	80	2.277	3.11	7.6	10.4	80.0	2.11	7.0
Copper	7	5	0.140	0.19	0.5	0.6	6.0	0.16	0.5
Zinc	107	75	2.137	2.92	7.1	9.7	57.0	1.50	5.0

Dr. Smart's Homemade Cat and Dog Food Recipes

Equipment Needed

- A food processor to process the ingredients.
- A kitchen scale that weighs in mg and kg or in ounces and pounds.
- A large bowl or container in which to mix the ingredients.
- Plastic bags or small containers to freeze daily meals in.
- Marking pencil to mark date made and number of meals on freezer bag or container.

Dr. Smart's Cat Food Recipe

65% composed of ground fresh fish (salmon, white fish, perch, pickerel), red meat (beef, lamb, wild game), or poultry (duck, turkey, or chicken), this food can be lightly sautéed or fed raw (I prefer to slightly cook the fish). If you want you can grind the soft ends of the chicken bones with cartilage attached, which will add calcium and other minerals, glucosamine, and chondroitin sulphate for joint support (if you do this, remove the shell from the eggs in the step below and discard before processing).

20% percent raw ground turkey, beef, or chicken livers, half of which could be chicken or turkey heart and/ or kidney (note: kidney this *must* be kept raw).

10% boiled egg plus shell.

1% dried spirulina herb, which can be purchased from a health food store

0.25% cod liver oil

0.25% flax seed oil or salmon oil

2% cider vinegar

Process and mix all ingredients together, weight out individual meals or a set number of meals and freeze in an appropriate container.

Guaranteed Analysis: Average Kcal/1000g=3880
(1450 Kcal/1000g as Fed)

	Dry Matter	as Fed		Dry Matter	as Fed
Min Protein %	50	18	Min Calcium %	1.00	0.55
Min. Fat %	18	6.5	Min P%	0.5	0.20
Moisture %	0	60			

Dr. Smart's Dog Food Recipe

40% ground meat (beef, lamb, bison, venison, pork etc), poultry (duck, chicken, turkey, etc.), or fish, or a combination of these ingredients. If allergies are a problem use only one source of meat. See the cat diet for further comments.

15% raw liver (beef, lamb, turkey, duck, chicken but not pork liver) heart and Kidney can also make up a portion.

8% hard boiled eggs plus shell.

10% fruits, largest proportions being apples, pears, melons, etc., and lesser amounts from blueberries, currants, raspberries, strawberries, etc. Also add a citrus fruit such as an orange or grapefruit. Choose different colors of fruit, remove large pits but leave the skins on all fruits, even the melons and the citrus fruit. Avoid grapes, rhubarb peach, and cherry pits

11% vegetables—a combination of colours, such as winter and summer squash, sweet potatoes, carrots, broccoli, green or yellow snap beans, etc. Do not remove the skins or the seeds. Avoid chard, spinach, onions.

5% long grain cooked brown rice (if concerned about grains, add more fruit and vegetables)

5% wheat germ

3% cider vinegar

1% spirulina dried

1% ground flax seed

0.5% extra virgin olive oil

0.5% garlic

Guaranteed Analysis: Average Kcal/1000g=3880 (1450 Kcal/1000g as Fed)

	Dry Matter	as Fed		Dry Matter	as Fed
Min Protein %	44	14	Min Calcium %	0.7	0.2
Min. Fat %	20	7	Min P%	0.4	0.1
Moisture %	0	70			

Feeding Directions

You must determine the number of calories required by your pet per day.

A normal, healthy, not obese 4 kg cat requires between 250 to 300 Kcal per day. The cat diet provides 1450 Kcal/1000g or 1.45 Kcal/g. Therefore this cat should be fed (250/1.45) or 170g of the diet per day

A healthy normal dog's calorie requirements can be determined by using the following formula: {(body weight in kilograms*30) + 70}*1. 8 = Kcal required per day, then calculate the grams of food per day, as in the example above for cats.

Genetically Engineered Foods and Pet Health Issues

One of the biggest challenges today in addressing human and animal health and various complex disease problems is in the accurate identification of causal factors responsible for illness. This is essential if effective government regulation, oversight, and preventive measures are to be implemented, and where feasible, appropriate treatments.

Possible causal factors in some of the health problems commonly occurring in companion animals include thousands of chemicals and synthetic organic compounds derived from various industrial and agricultural sources and which variously enter the environment, and what is eaten, drunk, and inhaled.

Recent toxicological advances have identified certain effects of these substances on the body, such as endocrine (hormonal) and metabolic (obesogenic and diabetogenic) disruption, as well as causing cancer, mutationsm and birth defects, notably herbicides like glyphosate, the main ingredient in Monsanto's Roundup herbicide, compounds like the phthalates and Bisphenyl A in plastics and food containers, the omnipresent flame-retardant bromide compounds (PBDEs), and dioxins and PCBs.

Now when it comes to making a risk assessment of genetically modified (GM) / genetically engineered food ingredients, primarily derived from herbicide resistant crops (and therefore containing herbicide residues as well as endogenously produced insecticide like Bt), supporters of such biotechnology are quick to point out that because so many chemical compounds already contaminate our environment, bodies, and food, you just can't prove that GM crops and food are harmful. Controlled laboratory animal studies, like those summarized by Smith (2007) and Fox (2011) are too often dismissed as not being relevant to real-life conditions, and if there were adverse health consequences, they would be readily diagnosed since GM crops and foods are now being grown and consumed globally.

In their recent review, Dona & Arvanitoyannis (2009) conclude that "The results of most of the rather few studies conducted with GM foods indicate that they may cause hepatic, pancreatic, renal, and reproductive effects and may alter hematological, biochemical, and immunologic parameters the significance of which remains unknown. The above results indicate that many GM foods have some common toxic effects. Therefore, further studies should be conducted in order to elucidate the mechanism dominating this action. Small amounts of ingested DNA may not be broken down under digestive processes and there is a possibility that this DNA may either enter the bloodstream or be excreted, especially in individuals with abnormal digestion as a result of chronic gastrointestinal disease or with immunodeficiency."

In a study analyzing the effects of genetically modified foods on mammalian health, researchers found that three varieties of Monsanto's GM corn—Mon 863, insecticide-producing Mon 810, and Roundup® herbicide-absorbing NK 603—approved for consumption by US, European, and several other national food safety authorities, caused liver, kidney, and other internal organ damage when fed to rats. Researchers J.S. de Vendomois and co-workers summarized these findings as follows:

"Effects were mostly concentrated in kidney and liver function, the two major diet detoxification organs, but in detail differed with each GM type. In addition, some effects on heart, adrenal, spleen, and blood cells were also frequently noted. As there normally exists sex differences in liver and kidney metabolism, the highly statistically significant disturbances in the function of these organs, seen between male and female rats, cannot be dismissed as biologically insignificant as has been proposed by others. We therefore conclude that our data strongly suggests that these GM maize varieties induce a state of hepatorenal toxicity.... These substances have never before been an integral part of the human or animal diet and therefore their health consequences for those who consume them, especially over long time periods are currently unknown."

Beyond the uncertainty and precautionary principles, human and veterinary *evidence-based medicine* can help raise or lower probabilities when it comes to making objective risk determinations of new drugs, vaccines, GM foods, and various chemical contaminants and adulterants.

My assertion that GM pet food ingredients can be a health risk to dogs and cats is based on the increasing number of letters that I have been receiving from readers of my nationally syndicated *Animal Doctor* newspaper column in the U.S., whose animals are suffering from what attending veterinarians are diagnosing and treating as allergies, atopic dermatitis, irritable bowel syndrome, and inflammatory bowel disease/colitis. (See Postscript below). I have been writing this weekly column for over 40 years, and the increase in letters dealing with these kinds of health problems in dogs and cats began around the mid 1990s when GM crop acreage began to explode and more and more of the ingredients in livestock feed and pet foods were derived from such crops.

This assertion is supported by the evidence-based medicine of health improvement following a change in diet. Afflicted animals' symptoms were often quickly resolved when they were transitioned onto a diet containing no GM ingredients. Their often reported increased vitality and healthfulness would imply some impairment of metabolism and immune system function had been rectified by a change in diet and improved nutrition.

This assertion that pet food ingredients derived from GM corn and soy can pose a significant health hazard to companion animals is further supported by the fact that other potential disease co-factors in the background of companion animals have, to my knowledge, remained relatively constant over the years, with no significant market increase in the use of agricultural pesticides, with the exception of glyphosate, of animal insecticides and anti-parasite drugs, while the frequency rates of cat and dog vaccinations have actually begun to decline.

Many of the pathophysiological, anatomical, and developmental changes documented in laboratory animals fed GM foods may be eventually identified by veterinary pathologists and immunologists doing detailed forensic and toxicological studies of diseased, dying, and dead companion animals. But currently such research, to the best of my knowledge, is neither being conducted nor funded. So I advise both consumers and pet care-givers to avoid all foods derived from GM crops because the findings of evidence-based medicine support the growing consensus that such foods are unsafe and not fit for man or beast.

It is not illegal in the U.S. for food and beverage manufacturers to make the legitimized claim "No GM" ingredients or "GM-Free" on their packaging to indicate that no ingredients come from genetically engineered food sources. In all the European countries and in Australia, New Zealand, Japan, South Korea, Brazil, and other countries, there is mandatory labeling for all produce containing GM crop ingredients, but not in the U.S. So I see no reason why some enlightened pet food manufacturer in the U.S. should not set the ball rolling and make the legitimate claim of being GM-free. The Non-GMO Project is becoming the standard for verifying the non-GMO status of food products. Many companies are putting their products through the Project's verification program, and a Non-GMO Project verified claim on pet foods would be the most credible claim a pet food company could make regarding the absence of GM material.

I can see no legitimate reason for those manufactured pet foods containing no ingredients from genetically engineered food sources to not be labeled "GM-Free" unless there is some tacit agreement within the industry to not do so. In which case, I would say that it is time to break ranks and for those pet food manufacturers who can make a legitimate claim, to indicate such on their pet food containers. To not do so is to abdicate corporate responsibility to inform consumers who have a right to know; and to conform to the overarching ethos of the U.S. and multinational agribusiness food and drug alliance (FDA), and related government de-regulating agencies, that continues to whitewash public concern, deny a growing scientific consensus, and dismiss evidence-based medicine that consumables that include GM ingredients are safe for neither man nor beast.

Supportive References

1. de Vendômois, J.S., Roullier, F., Cellier, D., Séralini, G.E. A Comparison of the Effects of Three GM Corn Varieties on Mammalian Health. *Int J Biol Sci* 5:706–726, 2009

2. Dona, A. and Arvanitoyannis, I.S., Health Risks of Genetically Modified Foods. *Critical Reviews in Food Science and Nutrition* 49: 164–175, 2009

3. Domingo, J. L. Toxicity Studies of Genetically Modified Plants: A Review of the Published Literature. *Critical Reviews in Food Science and Nutrition* 47:8, 721–733, 2007

4. Fox, M.W. *Healing Animals and the Vision of One Health.* Tallevast, FL One Health Vision Press/Amazon.com 2011.

5. Pusztai, A., Bardocz, S., and Ewen, S. W. B. Genetically Modified Foods: Potential Human Health Effects. In: *Food Safety: Contaminants and Toxins* (ed) D'Mello JPF CAB International, Wallingford Oxon, UK, pp 347–372, 2003.

6. Seralino, G.E., et al. Genetically modified crops safety assessments: present limits and possible improvements. *Environmental Sciences Europe* 23:10–19, 2011 .

7. Smith, J.M. *Genetic Roulette: The Documented Health Risks of Genetically Engineered Foods Fairfield.* Iowa Yes! Books 2007.

8. Traavik, T., and Heinemann, J. Genetic Engineering and Omitted Health Research: Still No Answers to Ageing Questions. *TWN Biotechnology & Biosafety* Series 7, 2007.

9. Wilson, A.K, Latham, J.R., andSteinbrecher, R.A. Transformation-induced mutations in transgenic plants: Analysis and biosafety implications. *Biotechnology and Genetic Engineering Reviews* 23: 209–226, 2006.

10. Zhang, L. et. al. Exogenous plant MIR168a specifically targets mammalian LDLRAP1: evidence of cross-kingdom regulation by microRNA. *Cell Research* doi:10.1038/cr.2011.158, 2011.

For additional information, visit www.non-gmoreport.com and also www.nongmoproject.org.

DENTAL PROBLEMS IN DOGS AND CATS

Until recently, dental problems in cats and dogs were a neglected aspect of home pet care. These problems include the build up of tartar or scale on the teeth, gum inflammation, gingivitis, stomatitis, and serious periodontal disease and tooth-root abscesses. Not only do affected pets develop nauseating halitosis and find it painful to eat, the inflammation in their mouths can result in the spread of bacteria in their blood streams to internal organs, along with inflammatory substances called cytokines. These can damage the heart, causing serious and often fatal heart disease, as in humans with severe peridontitis, and also harm the kidneys, pancreas, liver, and other internal organs.

These inflammatory substances are also produced from body fat in overweight and obese animals, just as in humans. Obesity and dental problems are associated with highly processed manufactured pet foods, especially those high in cereals, and can lead to heart, kidney, liver, and joint inflammation, pancreatic disease and related digestive problems, Type 11 diabetes, and other health problems, including increased susceptibility to infections and allergies because the animals' immune systems are impaired.

A few drops of fish oil like Nordic Naturals (1 teaspoon daily for a cat or 30 lbs. dog, 1 tablespoon for larger dogs) in the pet's food every day will help reduce gum inflammation. Getting the animal used to having very strong organic green tea, or some dry tea leaves rubbed nightly on the gums and between the teeth, may help stop plaque accumulation and help in the treatment of canine and feline periodontal disease. Such treatment has been recommended for oral cancer and caries in humans. The oral gel made by PetzLife Oral Care Products (www.petzlife.com) is an excellent product that loosens scale/tartar, helps reduce inflammation and infection, and can reduce the risks of and need for dental surgery.

Pet Food Research Methods

The design of a nutritional study determines how significant or relevant the tested diets are in caring for a pet with a specific health problem. The following research designs are listed in order of importance. These have been modified from the original to be applicable to veterinary clinical nutrition (Figure 1). These guidelines provide both the consumer and the veterinarian with a set of criteria to critically evaluate the research associated with veterinary medical foods and determine if the product is truly efficacious.

Level 1: Randomized controlled studies

A group of similar animals housed under the same conditions are fed diets over the same time frame, one a control diet, and the other(s) with intentional modifications of that diet.

In most trials, the animals are randomly assigned to control and treatment groups. Predetermined, routine clinical examinations of each animal are conducted, and tests run to measure the clinical and metabolic response of the animals to these diets. The results are then analyzed by what is considered to be the most appropriate statistical program, then the results are interpreted and conclusions drawn. Many variations of these trials exist. To eliminate biases the most common are blind studies were the people who are feeding, collecting and analyzing the data are not aware of which diet they are feeding to any given animal.

Level 2: Prospective Studies

In a prospective study pets with a specific problem that meets a specific set of clinical signs and metabolic changes are selected.

These patients are divided into several groups and specific diet(s) are fed. Changes in their clinical and metabolic condition are monitored over a set period using predetermined clinical and analytical criteria established in the research protocol. A control diet or control group may be included. These are pets and are not kept for the trial period in a research facility but at home, so patient/owner compliance becomes an issue.

Level 3: Retrospective Studies

Retrospective studies are common in companion animal nutrition. These studies utilize the owner's recall of events and the medical records of a group of animals with the same or similar condition. The history and records are analyzed to determine if there are any common threads within this information that can lead to problem identification and determination of associated risk factors. Conclusions are then drawn, and eventually solutions found. Formally, these are epidemiology studies and are by far the cheapest to do.

Level 4: Third Person Research

A knowledgeable individual or a group of specialists review, interpret and summarize pertinent published literature on a particular topic. Conclusions are drawn and recommendations made. The findings are published in a journal as a review article or in books. The 2006 NRC nutrient requirements for dogs and cats and the AAFCO nutrient profiles for dogs and cats used by the industry to define and develop complete and balanced diets are examples of this type of research. Corporate biases can strongly influence literature selection.

Most of the industry's preliminary dietary formulations were done using this method. A successful diet coupled with market-demand determinations, help secure the financial resources for further product development.

Level 5: Case-Control Studies

For these studies, the histories of patients with a certain condition are compared to those without that problem. In veterinary medicine, the researcher is dependent on the owners to provide a reliable history for both the study and the control group. Once enough cases are collected and similar results found, the researcher may write a review article following a scientifically proven path, and/or design a prospective, or a retrospective study to support the case findings. Randomized control studies are the next level up where the hypotheses are drawn from the previous studies, and tested in a more controlled environment.

Level 6: A Series of Case Reports or a Single Case

Report

These are generally the first step in developing a research hypothesis. They represent a case or a series of cases that are unique and respond to a particular diet. If these are not published as case reports, they are regarded as anecdotal evidence, and therefore of limited value. These are considered the lowest level validation.

Level 7: Educated Ideas, Editorials, and Opinions

Although these are not regarded as scientific, initially most veterinary diets were developed and marketed based on these more subjective criteria.

Validation of Research

Within the scientific community, none of these research trials is considered valid unless published in a forum that requires peer review and approval prior to publication. This process relies on the integrity and policies of the journal's editorial board and the reviewers. To accomplish this can take a considerable amount of time.

Corporate biases can weaken the validity of nutritional research by promoting studies with a positive effect and ignoring those showing a negative trend, or by amalgamating several weak positive studies to produce one strong positive result. Another concern is if the company's research and development division is interested in supporting a particular conclusion, studies showing negative results may be excluded. Positive trends rather than statistically sound results are cited as positive research in support of a new dietary formulation and its efficacy. In order to properly evaluate a company's research the reader must be satisfied that corporate bias did not exist in the formulation or in the marketing of a veterinary medical food. This may be almost impossible to determine from the information provided by the company.

Confidentiality dictates what research supported by pet food company's is published in peer-reviewed journals. They may also seek to bypass this step by holding or sponsoring conferences/symposia, and by publishing fact sheets where non-peer reviewed research and the preliminary results of research studies are presented.

Academia

Let us examine how long this research process can take within an academic institution, when nonindustry independent funding is available through grant competitions:

Step 1: Establishing the hypotheses to test, designing the experiment, getting animal care approval, and writing and applying for grants to fund the nutritional research project can take from two to twelve months.

Step 2: The wait for funding approval depends on the deadlines for grant submissions, but the wait can be between two to four months.

Step 3: Upon approval the trial must be set up, and this includes establishing the facilities, purchasing the animals, notifying the testing centers when their services are required, and hiring graduate students and technical help to run the trials. If this can be expedited, the time frame could be as short as a month or as long as four months.

Up to this point, between five and twenty months have passed, without a bite of food being eaten by test subjects!

Step 4: The length of the actual trial, including a period of adjustment, depends on the hypotheses, but will likely be between six to thirty-six months. The ideal period would be over the lifetime of the pet of ten to fourteen years. During this time, as the data are being collected, the results received can be collated and preliminary analyses done.

Step 5: All the data are collected, statistically analyzed, interpreted and put into a format suitable for publication. Depending on how well organized the principle researcher is and the availability of graduate students to do a literature search and writing, this process can take between three to twelve months to complete.

Step 6: The actual peer review of the report, manuscript corrections, and publication of the research can take between six months and eighteen months to complete, or the research can be permanently stalled at this step. One of the major obstacles is when the reviewers of the research findings submit diametrically opposed corrections and/or recommendations. Then the research paper may be rejected for publication and never see the light of day.

Under ideal conditions, this whole process from step one to six can take from thirteen to sixty-six months to complete.

The Corporate Sector

Within the corporate sector, how long this process can take is not so easy to determine. What we do know, or are told, is that research and development is a big budget item. What we are not told is what percentage of that is allocated to pure scientific research into the development and efficacy of their veterinary prescription diets, and what is allocated to the research and development into factors that improve product profitability, such as new marketing strategies, new packaging, improved manufacturing methods, flavor development, etc. One company has a whole department, headed by an engineer with a Ph.D., devoted to research into new packaging that is acceptable and convenient for the consumer, maintains the shelf life of the food under the most adverse of conditions, and is easy and economical to ship.

All of the companies maintain state-of-the-art companion animal facilities where non-invasive studies related to diet palatability, digestibility, and ingredient preferences are done. In some facilities, dogs are also being trained to assist people with special needs. Each facility is a showcase and a window through which the public is allowed look and judge the company. The motives and power that drives the multinational corporations, and the marketing strategies used to sell their products, are evident. Invasive studies on animals, distressing to most pet lovers, are now generally outsourced to contract research facilities that may even be located abroad.

Figure 1: The Evidence Pyramid. Adapted for evaluating the research associated with the efficacy of veterinary medical foods

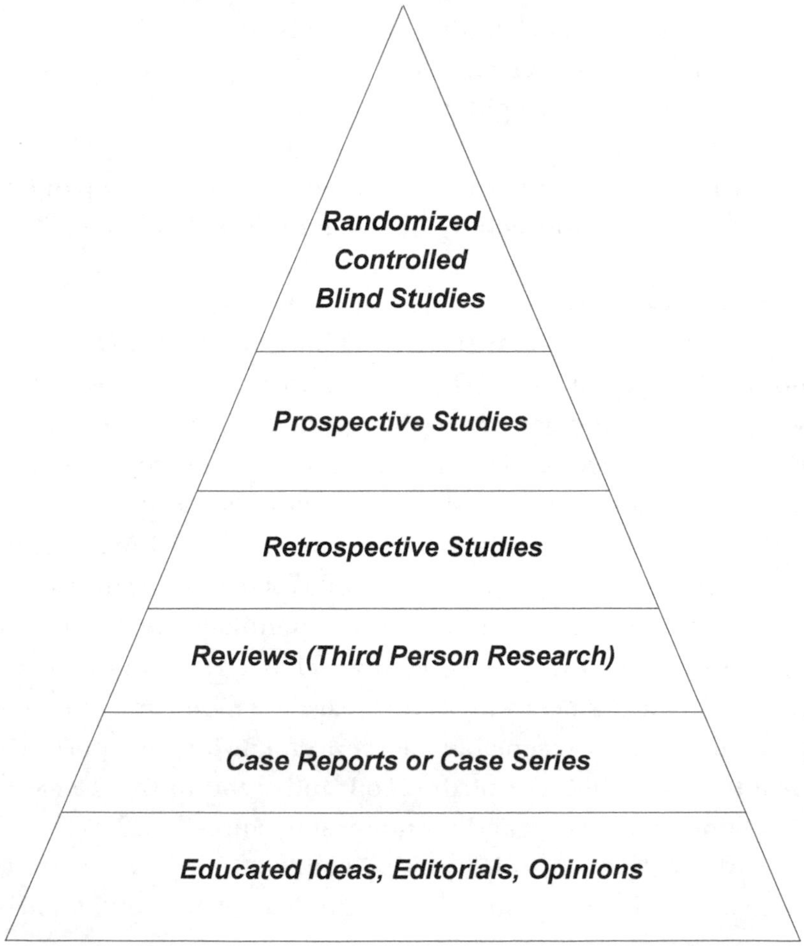

Randomized
Controlled
Blind Studies

Prospective Studies

Retrospective Studies

Reviews (Third Person Research)

Case Reports or Case Series

Educated Ideas, Editorials, Opinions

Dog and Cat
Vaccination Protocols

"Anytime you inject anything into a patient you have the potential of killing them."
—Professor Ron Schultz, D.V.M.

The practice of giving dogs and cats several different vaccinations against various diseases all at the same time early in life and then again every year as "boosters" for the rest of their lives is coming to a close. This is for two primary reasons: Animals can have adverse reactions to vaccinations that can impair their health for the rest of their lives; routine booster shots are not needed since earlier vaccinations have given animals sufficient immunity to the diseases in question.

First, the very young, i.e. before twelve weeks of age, kittens and puppies should not be given vaccinations since this can interfere with the natural immunity in their systems conferred by the colostrum or first milk of their mothers. But if the immune status of the mother is unknown, as is the situation for many to-be-adopted pups and kittens in animal shelters, vaccinations at an earlier age between five and six weeks is the usual protocol.

Adult animals in a compromised immune state, for example those who are ill, injured, or being given an anesthetic, are pregnant or nursing, or are old and infirm should not be vaccinated.

Rabies vaccinations, unless in-field conditions make this logistically difficult, should never be given at the same time other combined vaccinations are given. Separate by at least three weeks.

The following protocols for vaccinating dogs and cats have been published in the *American Holistic Veterinary Medical Association Journal.*

• The Minimum Vaccine Protocol for cats is at 12 weeks or older to give the so called "core" vaccinations FVR (herpes/rhinotracheitis) and FPV (feline parvovirus or panleukopenia), and then rabies 3-4 weeks later, but only if the antirabies vaccination is required by law. PureVac, canary pox vectored rabies vaccine (Merial) is preferred for cats. Vaccinating against Giardia is not advised since the vaccine can cause granulomas.

• FIV (feline immunodeficiency virus), FIP (feline infectious peritonitis) and Bordetella-kennel cough vaccinations are not recommended.

• FeLV (feline leukemia) vaccine should only be given to at-risk cats (such as indoor-outdoor cats) at 9 and 12 weeks, or 12 and 15 weeks with a booster at a year of age and none thereafter in order to reduce the chances of injection-site fibrosarcoma, a cancer that can be fatal. Aluminum hydroxide, an adjuvant in many vaccines, has been given a Class 4 carcinogenesis rating by the World Health Organization. Merial's Purevax Canary pox vectored feline leukemia vaccine is the safest and recommended because it does not contain this adjuvant.

• Cats should have serum titer tests for FPV later in life to determine their immune status. All vaccinations to be injected under the skin should be placed as far down the cat's limbs as possible since it is more difficult to treat fibrosarcomas that develop at other sites such as the neck and back.

The American Association of Feline Practitioners Feline Vaccination Panel's recommendation of early-age, repeated vaccinations is based on the fact that kittens respond differently when vaccinated because they have different levels of circulating antibodies from their mothers' milk that can interfere with the immune response triggered by vaccination. But I consider this protocol excessive and the risks, costs, and stress on kittens unjustified unless they are at risk in poorly managed breeding facilities and pet stores.

• The Minimum Vaccination Protocol for dogs is at 12 weeks or older to give MLV (modified live virus) distemper, hepatitis (Adenovirus-2) and parvovirus enteritis, and none thereafter. At

12-16 weeks, give rabies vaccination and then only every three years if permitted by law. (State and municipal laws that do not permit the use of a 3-year rabies vaccination should be challenged and changed).

• Corona virus and giardia vaccinations for dogs are not recommended. For dogs at risk, Leptospirosis vaccine (the four-serovar product of Fort Dodge being preferred) should be given at 12 and 15 weeks and repeated one year later. It only confers protection, however, for three to four months, so repeated vaccinations are called for with dogs with significant exposure risk.

• Lyme vaccine should be given to at-risk dogs but the bacterium vaccine can cause immune-complex disease so Merial's recombinant Lyme vaccine is preferred. Again, blood serum titers should be taken to assess dog's immune status where there is doubt, rather than simply giving booster shots. Neither Lyme disease vaccinations, that give highly unreliable protection, and leptospirosis vaccinations should be given close to the time that any other vaccinations are given.

• Studies have shown that in normal, healthy dogs at the time of vaccination, Parvovirus vaccines are good for seven years, rabies vaccines for three to seven years, Distemper vaccines for five to fifteen years (depending on the strain), and Adenovirus two vaccines for seven to nine years.

• If your cat or dog received all core vaccines by 16 weeks of age and you have reservations about revaccinations, have antibody blood titers evaluated at 1 year of age.

Professor Ron Schultz recommends using Merial's 3-way combo; parvo, distemper and CAV2/hepatitis as the only relatively safe combination of vaccines. No vaccine can guarantee immunity, since different strains of infective agents may be involved, and animals who are stressed, suffering from poor nutrition, genetic susceptibility and concurrent disease may have impaired immune systems and lowered resistance to disease. But this does not mean that they should never be vaccinated or be routinely revaccinated just in case, because vaccinations can cause further immune system impairment and a host of health problems—the so called vaccinosis diseases—that these new vaccination protocols are aimed at minimizing.

To find a holistic veterinarian in your area, a searchable list can be found at the website of the American Holistic Veterinary Medical Association: **http://www.ahvma.org**. Veterinarians wishing to learn more are encouraged to become members of the AHVMA.

Notes and References

A compendium of helpful links and resources for those wishing to conduct further research.

Chapter 1: An Introduction to What You Are Feeding Your Pet

1. N. G. Barnes (2004), A market analysis of the U.S. pet food industry to determine new opportunities for the cranberry industry (thesis), Center for Business Research, University of Massachusetts.
2. Product safety and alternative pet foods: North American market outlook, July 2007 (see: www.marketresearch.com/Packaged-Facts-v768/Product-Safety-Alternative-Pet-Foods-1499072).
3. Pet population data, Pet Food Institute, October, 15, 2006.
4. M. Smart (2007), Survey of accredited veterinary colleges for curriculum review, May 2007, unpublished.
5. M. Smart, S. Abood , C. Kirk, and M. Nixon (2007), Current issues in small animal nutrition course, Veterinary Information Network transcript.
6. T. Parker-Pope (November 3, 1997), Why vets recommend 'designer' chow, *The Wall Street Journal.*
7. 2005–2006 APPMA National Pet Owners Survey, American Pet Product Manufacturers Asssociation (see: www.americanpetproducts.org/newsletter/may2005/npos.html).
8. G. Aldrich (2007), Chicken first: Marketing ploy or quality enhancement?, PetFoodIndustry.com.
General reference:
1. www.petfoodindustry-digital.com/petfoodindustry/201206#pg1
2. www.petnutritionbysmart.blogspot.com

Chapter 2: The Largest Pet Food Recall Ever

1. AVMA Legislative Agenda (2007), Non-economic damages,

animals' legal status, *JAVMA* 230:1436.

2. V. Wensley Koch (2007), Letter to the editor, *JAVMA* 231:196.

3. Quote (2007) from *The Veterinary Record* 160:603.

Chapter 3: Pet Foods: A Veterinary and Ethical Evaluation

1. See: M. W. Fox (1997), *Eating with Conscience: The Bioethics of Food*, Troutdale, Oregon: NewSage Press; also see: M. W. Fox (1996) *Agricide: The Hidden Farm and Food Crisis that Affects Us All, 2d ed.*, Malabar, Florida: Krieger Publishing Company.

2. J. Corbin (1994), Pet foods and feeding, *Feedstuffs* 20: 86–90.

3. Editorial (May 20, 1996), *Food and Chemical News*, p.34.

4. W. Jean Dodds (1997), Pet food preservatives and other additives, *Complementary and Alternative Medicine*, A.M. Schoen and S.G.Wynne, eds. St. Louis: Mosby, 73–79.

5. W. Jean Dodds and S. Donohue (1994), Interactions of clinical nutrition with genetics, *The Waltham Book of Clinical Nutrition of the Dog and Cat*, Oxford: Pergamon Press.

6. W. Jean Dodds (1994), Nutritional influences on immune and thyroid function, *Proceedings of the American Holistic Veterinary Medical Association*, p 47.

7. H. Pasternak (2001), *Optimum Nutrition for Dogs and Cats: Nature's Amazing Miracle Cures*, Pacific Palisades, CA: Highland Veterinary Hospital publication.

8. K. S. Swanson (2006), Nutrient-gene interactions and their role in complex diseases in dogs, *JAVMA* 228:1513–1520.

9. Lon D. Lewis et al (1990), *Small Animal Clinical Nutrition III*, Topeka, Kansas: Mark Morris Associates.

10. Paul D. Pion et al (1992), Clinical findings in cats with dilated cardiomyopathy and relationship of findings to taurine deficiency, *JAVMA* 201:267–74.

11. Donald Strombeck (1998), *Home-Prepared Dog and Cat Diets: The Healthful Alternative*, Ames, IA: Iowa State University Press.

12. M. W. Fox (1971), *Integrative Development of Brain and Behavior in the Dog*, Chicago: University of Chicago Press, 186–191.

13. Editorial (1998), Consumer Union pet food story raises profession's hackles, *DVM Newsmagazine* 29: 1, 3.

14. J. E. Bower, et al. (1999), Effects of dietary fat and polyunsaturated fatty acids in dogs with naturally developing renal failure, *JAVMA* 215: 1588–1591.

15. R. W. Lacey (1993), Disease Transfer (chapter 21) in *Farm Animals and the Environment*, C. Philips and D. Piggins, eds. London: CAB International.

16. E. Tareke et al. (1999), Analysis of acrylamide, a carcinogen formed in heated foodstuffs, *J Agric. Food Chem* 14: 4998–5006.

17. C. H. Edinboro et al (2004), Epidemiologic study of relationships between consumption of canned commercial food and risk of hyperthyroidism in cats, *JAVMA* 224: 879–886.

18. K. A. Stenske et al (2006), Aflatoxicosis in dogs and dealing with suspected contamination in commercial foods, *JAVMA* 228: 1686–1691; and M. C. K. Leung et al. (2006), Mycotoxins in pet food: a review on worldwide prevalence and preventive strategies, *J Agric Food Chem* 54: 9623–9635.

19. J. T. LeJeune and D. D. Hancock (2001), Public health concerns associated with feeding raw meat diets to dogs, *JAVMA* 219 : 1222–1225.

20. M. W. Fox (196), Veterinary bioethics, *JAVMA* 208:1628–29; see also: M. W. Fox (1997), Veterinary bioethics in *Complementary and Alternative Veterinary Medicine*, A. M. Schoen and S. G. Wynne, eds. St. Louis: Mosby, p. 673–678; also see: M. W. Fox (2001), *Bringing Life to Ethics: Global Bioethics for a Humane Society* Albany: New York: State University of New York Press and M.W. Fox (1990), *Inhumane Society: The American Way of Animal Exploitation*, New York: St. Martin's Press.

21. Paul B. Thompson (1997), *Food Biotechnology in Ethical Perspective*, London: Chapman Hall.

22. M. W. Fox, (2004), *Killer Foods: What Scientists Do To Make Better Is Not Always Best*, Guilford, Connecticut: The Lyons Press

23. For example, see Virginia Worthington (2001) Nutritional quality of organic versus conventional fruits, vegetables, and grains, *J of Alternative and Complementary Medicine* 7): 161–173; and Bob Smith (2001), Organic foods vs. supermarket foods: element levels, *J Applied Nutrition* 45: 35–39.

Chapter 4: Digestiblity, Bioavailability, and all that Academic Stuff

1. H. S. Hussein (1999), Pet food applications of inulin and oligo-fructose, *Journal of Nutrition* 129 (7suppl.): 1454S-1456s.

Chapter 5: Veterinary Prescription Foods

1. L. M. Freeman (2007), Proceedings of the 25th American College of Veterinary Internal Medicine, Seattle Washington.
2. D. A. Dzanis (1999), Interpreting pet food labels—Special use petfoods, www.fda.gov/AnimalVeterinary/NewsEvents/FDAVet-erinarianNewsletter/ucm090102.htm.
3. J. Washburn (October 2007), Science under Siege: Private funding may be the greatest threat of all to scientific R&D: *Discover* 28 # 10: 66–73.
4. See: library.downstate.edu/EBM2/260.htm.
5. F. Jacob et al. (2002), Clinical evaluation of dietary modification for treatment of spontaneous chronic renal failure in dogs, *JAVMA* 220: 1163–1170.
6. D. Polzin (2003), Treating canine renal failure: evidence-based approach, Western Veterinary Conference.
7. J. E. Yaissle, C. Holloway, and T. Buffington (2004), Evaluation of owner education as a component of obesity treatment programs for dogs, *JAVMA* 224: 1932—1935.
8. C. M. Dorsten and D. M. Cooper (2004), Use of body condition scoring to manage body weight in dogs, *Contemp Top Lab Anim Sci* 43: 34–37.
9. C. R. L. Webster (2002), Nutritional management of liver disease (presentation), Tufts Animal Expo.
10. M. E. Smart, Comparative analyses of growth diets unpublished paper.
11. See: www.vohc.org/protocol.htm#2; see also F. Jacob et al. (2002), Clinical evaluation of dietary modification for treatment of spontaneous chronic renal failure in dogs , *JAVMA* 220: 1163–1170.

Chapter 6: The Predator Among Us: How Cats Are Unique

1. Elizabeth Hodgkins (2007), *Your Cat: Simple New Secrets To A Longer, Stronger Life*, New York: Thomas Dunne Books.

2. See www.catnutrition.org and linked references.

3. See www.catinfo.org.

4. Debra L. Zoran (December, 2002), Timely topics in nutrition: The carnivore connection to nutrition in cats, *JAVMA*, volume 221, number 11.

5. Ana Ruiz (2001), *The Spirit of Ancient Egypt*, New York: Algora Publishing.

6. Lon Lewis, Mark Morris, and Michael Hand (1987), *Small Animal Clinical Nutrition, 3rd ed.*, Topeka, KS: Mark Morris Institute.

7. James Morris and Quinton Rogers (1983), Nutritional implications of some metabolic anomalies of the cat, American Animal Association Proceedings, 325–331.

8. Stephan O'Brien and Warren Johnson (July, 2007), The evolution of cats, *Scientific American*, 68–75.

9. C. A. Buffington, D. J. Chew, et al. (January, 1997), Clinical evaluation of cats with nonobstructive urinary tract diseases, *JAVMA*, 46–50.

10. Justine Patrick (April, 2006), Deconstructing the regulatory facade: why confused consumers feed their pets ring dings and krispy kremes, Harvard Law School (see leda.law.harvard.edu/ leda/data/784/Patrick06.rtf).

Chapter 7: Diets for Healthy Cats: A Recipe for Disease?

1. Ann Martin (2003), *Foods Pets Die For, Shocking Facts About Pet Food*, Troutdale, OR: New Sage Press.

2. www.nzymes.com/Articles/whatsreallyinpetfoods.htm.

3. www.accessdata.fda.gov/scripts/petfoodrecall.

4. www.msnbc.msn.com/id/10771943.

5. www.news-medical.net/?id=29124.

6. dogblog.dogster.com/2007/06/06/texas-laboratory-finds-acetaminophen-in-pet-food/#more-3952.

7. www.preciouspets.org/truth.htm.

8. Paul Pion, Mark Kittleson, et al. (August, 1987), Myocardial failure in cats associated with low plasma taurine: A reversible cardiomyopathy, *Science*, 237(4816):764-8.

9. Elizabeth Hodgkins (2007), *Your Cat: Simple New Secrets To A Longer, Stronger Life*, New York: Thomas Dunne Books.

10. G. Frank, W. Anderson, et al. (2001), Use of a high protein diet in the management of feline diabetes mellitus, *Veterinary Therapeutics*, 2(3):238-46.

11. D. Panciera, et al (1990), Epizootiological patterns of diabetes mellitus in cats: 333 cases (1980–1986), *JAVMA*, 197(11):1504-8.

12. R. Nelson and L. Lewis (1990), Nutritional management of diabetes mellitus, *Seminars in Veterinary Medicine and Surgery (Small Animal)*, 5(3):178–186.

13. N. Bennet, D. Greco, et al. (2006), Comparison of a low carbohydrate-low fiber diet and a moderate carbohydrate-high fiber diet in the management of feline diabetes, *Journal of Feline Medicine and Surgery*, 8(2):73-84.

14. J. Rand, L. Fleeman, et al. (2004), Canine and feline diabetes mellitus: Nature or nurture?, *Journal of Nutrition*, 134(8 Suppl):2072S-2080S.

15. C. A. Buffington, Q. A. Rogers, and J. G. Morris (1985), Feline struvite urolitiasis: Magnesium effect depends on urinary pH, *Feline Practice*, 15:29–33.

16. C, Kirk, G. Ling, et al. (1995), Evaluation of factors associated with development of calcium oxalate urolitiasis in cats, *JAVMA*, 207.11:1429–1434.

17. M. Funaba, A. Uchiyama, et al. (2004), Evaluation of effects of dietary carbohydrate on formation of struvite crystals in urine and macromineral balance in clinically normal cats, *American Journal of Veterinary Research*, 65(2):138-42.

18. M. Funaba, T. Yamate, et al. (2003), Effects of a high-protein diet versus dietary supplementation with ammonium chloride on struvite crystal formation in urine of clinically normal cats, *American Journal of Veterinary Research*, 64(8):1059-64.

19. S. DiBartola, C. Buffington, et al. (1993), Development of chronic renal disease in cats fed a commercial diet, *JAVMA*, ;202(5):744-51.

20. C. Buffington, D. Chew, et al. (1997), Clinical evaluation of cats with nonobstructive urinary tract diseases, *JAVMA*, 210(1):46-50.
21. www.salon.com/news/feature/2007/05/24/pet_food.

Chapter 8: When Cat Foods Become Drugs: A Prescription for Disaster

1. Justine Patrick (April, 2006), Deconstructing the regulatory facade: why confused consumers feed their pets ring dings and krispy kremes, Harvard Law School (see leda.law.harvard.edu/leda/data/784/Patrick06.rtf).
2. Federal Food, Drug, and Cosmetic Act, Chapter 2, section 201(g)1(B).
3. Federal Food, Drug, and Cosmetic Act, Chapter 4, section 403(r)1(B), section 403(r)3.
4. Federal Food, Drug, and Cosmetic Act, Chapter 4, section 403(r)6.
5. Elizabeth Hodgkins (2007), *Your Cat: Simple New Secrets To A Longer, Stronger Life*, New York: Thomas Dunne Books.
6. C. A. Buffington, Q. A. Rogers, and J. G. Morris (1985), Feline struvite urolitiasis: Magnesium effect depends on urinary pH, *Feline Practice*, 15:29–33.
7. C, Kirk, G. Ling, et al. (1995), Evaluation of factors associated with development of calcium oxalate urolitiasis in cats, *JAVMA*, 207.11:1429–1434.
8. Prescription Diet® c/d® Multicare Feline, Hill's Pet Nutrition, Topeka, KS.
9. See patft.uspto.gov/netacgi/nph-Parser?Sect1=PTO1&Sect2= HITOFF&d=PALL&p=1&u=%2Fnetahtml%2FPTO%2Fsrchnum. htm&r=1&f=G&l=50&s1=6,203,825.PN.&OS=PN/6,203,825&RS= PN/6,203,825.
10. G. Frank, W. Anderson, et al. (2001), Use of a high protein diet in the management of feline diabetes mellitus, *Veterinary Therapeutics*, 2(3):238-46.
11. N. Bennet, D. Greco, et al. (2006), Comparison of a low carbohydrate-low fiber diet and a moderate carbohydrate-high fiber diet in the management of feline diabetes, *Journal of Feline*

Medicine and Surgery, 8(2):73-84.

12. J. Rand, L. Fleeman, et al. (2004), Canine and feline diabetes mellitus: Nature or nurture?, *Journal of Nutrition*, 134(8 Suppl):2072S-2080S.

13. Purina Veterinary Diets™ DM Diabetes Management™ Brand Formula, canned.

Chapter 9: Finding Our Way Back: A New Map For Feline Health

1. www.homevet.com/petcare/foodbook.html.

2. Paul Pion, Mark Kittleson, et al. (August, 1987), Myocardial failure in cats associated with low plasma taurine: A reversible cardiomyopathy, *Science*, 237(4816):764-8.

3. www.api4animals.org/facts.php?p=359&more=1.

4. Debra L. Zoran (December, 2002), Timely topics in nutrition: The carnivore connection to nutrition in cats, *JAVMA*, volume 221, number 11.

5. Stephan O'Brien and Warren Johnson (July, 2007), The evolution of cats, *Scientific American*, 68–75.

6. www.felinespride.com.

7. www.omaspride.com.

8. Justine Patrick (April, 2006), Deconstructing the regulatory facade: why confused consumers feed their pets ring dings and krispy kremes, Harvard Law School (see leda.law.harvard.edu/leda/data/784/Patrick06.rtf).

9. Elizabeth Hodgkins (2007), *Your Cat: Simple New Secrets To A Longer, Stronger Life*, New York: Thomas Dunne Books.

10. www.catnutrition.org.

Chapter 10: Future Foods: Genetically Engineered or Go Organic?

1. José L Domingo (2007), Toxicity studies of genetically modified plants: A review of the published literature, Critical Reviews in Food Science and Nutrition 47, 8 ; 721–733.

2. A. Dona and I. S. Arvanitoyannis (2009), Health risks of genetically modified foods, Critical Reviews in Food Science and Nutrition 49: 164–175.

3. S. W. B. Ewen and A. Pusztai (1999), Effect of diets
ing genetically modified potatoes expressing Galanthus
lectin on rat small intestine, Lancet 354: 1353–1354.

4. The rBGH bovine growth hormone (BST) has been prom.
ed globally by Monsanto in the full knowledge of science show
ing damage to both cattle and those who consume the milk
of cows treated with rBGH (for details, see: M. W. Fox (2004),
Killer Foods: What Scientists Do To Make Better Is Not Always
Best, Guilford, CT: The Lyons Press.)

5. The deaths of cattle in Hesse, Germany, have been linked
with Bt176 maize, but there appear to have been determined
efforts to "lose" key scientific information and to attribute the
cattle deaths to mismanagement and other factors (see:
www.i-sis.org.uk/CAGMMAD.php).

6. Broiler chickens fed on Chardon LL—the mortality rate was
twice as high as that of the control group (NB the infamous
case of Prof Alan Gray of ACRE and the failure of that Committee to examine evidence placed before it). See: www.i-sis.org.
uk/appeal.php.

7. Rats fed on Chardon LL—weight gain was much reduced
(see: www.i-sis.org.uk/appeal.php).

8. The work of the Norwegian scientist Terje Traavik and his
colleagues is on-going and has still to be published; see also:
Filipino islanders blame GM crop for mystery sickness. Monsanto denies scientist's claim that maize may have caused 100
villagers to fall ill—John Aglionby in Kalyong, southern Philip-
pines, The Guardian, 3 March 3, 2004 (see: www.guardian.co.uk/
gmdebate/Story/0,2763,1160789,00.html).

9. Allergic reactions and livestock deaths 2005 attributable to
Bt cotton in India (Madhya Pradesh) (see: news.webindia123.
com/news/showdetails.asp?id=170692&cat=Health).

10. Re the Monsanto rat feeding study on MON863 maize,
which the company was desperate to keep out of the public domain 2004 (see: www.seedsofdeception.com/utility/
showArticle/?objectID=221); (also see: Genetically Modified
Corn Study Reveals Health Damage and Cover-up, by Jeffrey M.
Smith, accessed at: news.independent.co.uk/world/science_

gy/story.jsp? story=640430); (also see: www.efsa.eu.int/
/gmo/gmo_opinions/381_en.html); (also see: www.
tch.org/archive2.asp?arcid=5270).

ffrey Smith's book, *Genetic Roulette*, documents more than 60 health risks of GM foods in easy-to-read, two-page spreads, and it demonstrates how current safety assessments are not competent to protect consumers from the dangers. Smith's previous book, *Seeds of Deception* (www.seedsofdeception.com), is the world's best-selling book on the subject.

"Spilling the Beans" is a monthly column available at www.responsibletechnology.org.

For additional documentation, see M.W. Fox (2011) *Healing Animals & the Vision of One Health*, CreatSpace Books/Amazon.com and visit **www.drfoxvet.com** for updated reviews of GMOs in pet foods and risks to animals of such genetically engineered ingredients.

Organic Agriculture References

1. C. Badgley, et al. (2007), Organic agriculture and the global food supply, *Renewable Agriculture and Food Systems* 22: 86–108.
2. M. W. Fox (1997), *The Boundless Circle: Caring For Creatures and Creation*, Wheaton, Illinois: Quest Books.
3. Henry Emmons (2006), *The Chemistry of Joy*, New York: Simon and Shuster.
4. For example, see Bob L. Smith (1993), Organic foods vs. supermarket foods: Element Levels, *Journal of Applied Nutrition* 45: 35–39; and Virginia Worthington (2001), Nutritional quality of organic versus conventional fruits and vegetables, *Journal of Complementary and Alternative Medicine* 7: 161–173.
5. See H. Steinfeld, P. Gerber, T. Wassenaer, V. Casetl. M. Rosales, and C. de Haan (2006), Livestock's Long Shadow, published by the United Nation's Food and Agriculture Organization, Washington, DC.

6. Organically certified foods of both animal and plant origin contain more essential nutrients, notably antioxidants, than conventionally grown produce, and, of course, cause less environmental harms and are pesticide free. For documentation, see J. Cooper , C. Leifert , and U. Niggily (eds.) (2007), *Handbook of Food Quality and Safety Cambridge*, UK: Woodhead Publ. Inc.

Chapter 11: Diet, Nutrition, Health and Behavior: Surveys and Overview

1. M. W. Fox (1997), Veterinary bioethics, pp 673-678 in Complementary and Alternative Medicine, A. M. Schoen and S. G. Wynn (eds.), St Louis: Mosby, 673–678.
2. American Association of Veterinarians for Animal Rights, Guide to Congenital and Hereditary Disorders in Dogs, P. O. Box 208, Davis, CA 95617-0208.
3. News/Companion Animals (2007), Top 10 reasons pets visit veterinarians, JAVMA 229, 651.
4. Alexandra Gorman (2007), Household Hazards: Potential Hazards of Home Cleaning Products. A report by the Women's Voice for the Earth. Note: a common flame retardant, polybrominated diphenyl ethers (PBDEs), used in carpet padding, fabrics, and mattresses has recently been linked by the U.S. Environmental Protection Agency with hyperthyriodism in cats (see: www.epa.gov/oppt/pbde).
5. For details, see M. W. Fox (2004), Killer Foods: What Scientists Do To Make Better Is Not Always Best Guilford, CT: The Lyons Press, Guilford.
6. News and reports (18 August 2007), Rats reveal risks of 'junk food' during pregnancy, The Veterinary Record, 215.
7. M. A. McMichael (2007), Oxidative stress, antioxidants, and assessment of oxidative stress in dogs and cats, JAVMA 231: 734–720.
8. P. Roudebush. et al. (2006), Nutritional management of brain-aging dogs, JAVMA 227: 722–728.
9. K. M. Heinemann and J. E. Bauer (2006), Docosahexaenoic acid and neurologic development in animals, JAVMA 228: 700–705.

Index

CPSIA information can be obtained
at www.ICGtesting.com
Printed in the USA
LVHW041614210819
628458LV00011B/804